BlockChain

for

Beginners

Matthew Smith

Table of Contents

Introduction 10

Chapter 1 – A History of Currency, Cryptocurrency, and Blockchain 15

    Money 16

    Cryptocurrency 17

    How Did Cryptocurrencies Develop? 18

    Predecessors to Blockchain 19

        DigiCash 19

        HashCash 21

        B-Money 22

        E-Gold 23

        Bitgold 25

    Blockchains 27

Chapter 2 - Blockchain Basics 30

    Components of a Blockchain 31

    Security Concerns 33

    Types of Blockchain 34

    Blockchain Technology Overview 36

    Centralization Example 38

    Decentralized Example 39

Chapter 3 - The Business of Blockchain 40

    Different Industries that Use Blockchain Technology 40

    Adding Value to Your Business 42

    Growing Money 45

    The Cloud and Blockchain 46

    Blockchain and Gaming 47

- Supply Chain Management and Blockchain 49
- Blockchain Technology and Quality Assurance 50
- Chapter 4 - Blockchain Career Opportunities 51
  - Blockchain Career Options 52
    - Blockchain Developer..52
    - Blockchain Quality Engineer 53
    - Blockchain Legal Consultants 54
    - Blockchain Designers 55
    - Blockchain Project Manager..55
    - Blockchain programmer...55
    - Blockchain Product Manager 56
    - Risk Analyst...56
    - Business Analyst 56
    - Crypto Community Manager 57
    - Blockchain jobs in Banking..57
    - Example job descriptions...58
  - Where are you able to find a blockchain job?........................68
  - Blockchain Career..69
  - Blockchain Career Opportunities – Conclusion 71
- Chapter 5 - Proof of labor vs. Proof of Stake 72
  - Proof of labor 72
  - Proof of Stake 75
  - Benefits of the Proof of Stake Model 77
  - Proof of Stake Challenges 79
- Chapter 6 - Benefits of Blockchain Technology 80
  - Eliminating Third Parties...81
  - Control Over Data..81

- Better Data Quality and Integrity 82
- Durability and Reliability 82
- The Integrity of knowledge Processing and Transfers 83
- Transparency and Auditability 83
- Faster Transactions 84
- Lower Transaction Costs 84

Chapter 7 - Decentralized Finance (DeFi) 86
- How is DeFi different from Bitcoin? 87
- How does DeFi work? 87
- What is a smart contract? 89
- Who created DeFi? 90
- What are you able to do with DeFi? 91
- How do people make money in DeFi? 92
- How risky is DeFi? 92

Chapter 8 - Smart Contracts 95
- What Is Smart Contract? 96
- Benefits of Smart Contracts 97
  - Trust and Transparency 98
  - Security 98
- How Do Smart Contracts Work? 99
- Smart Contacts and Flight Insurance 101
- Voting and Blockchain 102
- Blockchain Implementation of a smart contract and Crowdfunding 104
- Use Cases of Smart Contracts 106
- Amending and Terminating Smart Contracts 106
- The Limits of Incorporating Vagueness Into Smart Contracts 108

- Do Smart Contracts Guarantee Payment? 110
- Risk Allocation for Attacks and Failures 112
- Governing Law and Venue 113
- Best Practices 114
- Future of Smart Contracts 116

Chapter 9 - Blockchain Platforms... 118
- What is a blockchain platform?.. 118
- Ethereum Blockchain 118
  - How to make use of Ethereum 120
  - How to store Ether 122
  - There are various sorts of wallets. 122
  - How to buy Ether 124
  - How Ethereum Works 125
  - Ethereum Use Cases 129
  - How OriginStamp uses the Ethereum blockchain 131
- Hyperledger Blockchain 132
  - What is Hyperledger Fabric?... 132
  - What Hyperledger Fabric is not....................................... 135
  - Hyperledger Platforms... 135
  - Hyperledger Tools 136
  - A Note on Hyperledger and Cryptocurrency 138
  - Fabric Smart Contracts (Chaincode)................................ 139
  - Hyperledger Fabric Components 142
  - Peers (or Nodes) 143
  - Hyperledger Fabric CA 146
  - Fabric CA Diagram 147
  - Ledger 147

- Hyperledger Fabric Workflow 149
- Transaction Processing 149
- R3 Corda Blockchain 152
  - What is R3 and Corda? 152
  - The R3 Corda Vision 153
  - Blockchain Benefits 154
  - The Benefits of DeFi 155
  - Blockchain and Distributed Ledger Technology 156
  - Is Corda a Blockchain? 158
  - R3 Corda Programs 158
  - R3 Corda Features 162
  - Permissioned vs. Permissionless Blockchains 163
  - Libertarian Dreams vs. Regulated Reality 163
  - R3 Corda's Privacy Option 164
  - Understanding ISO 166
  - R3 and CBDCs? 166
  - Corda, XDC, XLM, and XRP 168
  - Corda's Future Ecosystem 169
- Quorum Blockchain 170
  - Need for Quorum Blockchain 170
  - Defining Quorum Blockchain 171
  - A singular shared blockchain 173
  - Architecture of Quorum Blockchain 174
  - Who is Using Quorum? 175
  - Top 10 Quorum Blockchain Use Cases 176
  - How Does Quorum Achieve Consensus? 189
  - Data Privacy- The assets of Quorum 190

    The Working of Quorum - Private Transactions and Smart Contracts 191

    Validation of Blocks and State Consensus...................... 194

Chapter 10 - Risks and Challenges of Blockchain Technology 196

    Major Hurdles of Blockchain 199

    Risks of Blockchain Technology 200

Chapter 11 - Deciding if Blockchain Technology is a correct choice for You 202

    Know Who is going to be watching Your Data 203

    Writeable Data 203

    Data Alteration 204

    Data Restoration 205

    Easy to Share 206

    Storage Limitations 207

    Verification Process 207

    Taking subsequent Step 208

Chapter 12 - Blockchain Implementation Mistakes to Avoid....211

    Having Unrealistic Expectations 211

    Underestimating the Time Commitment 213

    Being Impatient 214

    Not Limiting Access 215

Conclusion.. 216

Additional Learning Resources 217

    Online Training... 217

        Online Degree™ in Blockchain 217

        Online Degree™ in Blockchain for Business................... 218

        Certified Blockchain Expert™.. 219

Certified Blockchain Architect™ 221

Certified Smart Contract Developer™ 222

Certified Blockchain and Finance Professional™ 223

Certified Blockchain Security Expert (CBSE) 224

Certified Enterprise Blockchain Architect (CEBA) 225

6-Figure Blockchain Developer 227

Become a Blockchain Developer 227

Certified Ethereum Expert™ 228

Certified Ethereum Developer™ 229

Certified Hyperledger Expert™ 230

Certified Quorum Expert™ 231

Certified Corda Expert™ 232

Build a Blockchain and a Cryptocurrency from Scratch .. 233

Ethereum Blockchain Developer Bootcamp With Solidity (2022) 234

Blockchain Development on Hyperledger Fabric using Composer 235

Books 236

Blockchain By Example: A developer's guide to creating decentralized applications using Bitcoin, Ethereum, and Hyperledger 236

Mastering Blockchain: A deep dive into distributed ledgers, consensus protocols, smart contracts, DApps, cryptocurrencies, Ethereum, and more, 3rd Edition 237

Blockchain with Hyperledger Fabric: Build decentralized applications using Hyperledger Fabric 2, 2nd Edition 238

Blockchain Development with Hyperledger: Build decentralized applications with Hyperledger Fabric and Composer 239

Hands-On Blockchain Development in 7 Days: Create a decentralized gaming application using Ethereum 240

Mastering Blockchain: A deep dive into distributed ledgers, consensus protocols, smart contracts, DApps, cryptocurrencies, Ethereum, and more, 3rd Edition 241

Blockchain Development for Finance Projects: Building next-generation financial applications using Ethereum, Hyperledger Fabric, and Stellar 242

Hands-On Cybersecurity with Blockchain: Implement DDoS protection, PKI-based identity, 2FA, and DNS security using Blockchain 244

Blockchain Quick Start Guide: A beginner's guide to developing enterprise-grade decentralized applications .245

Learn Blockchain Programming with JavaScript: Build your very own Blockchain and decentralized network with JavaScript and Node.js 246

Building Blockchain Projects: Building decentralized Blockchain applications with Ethereum and Solidity 247

Bibliography 249

Index 252

About the Author 254

Dedication 256

Introduction

> *"The journey of a thousand miles begins with one step."*
> - Lao Tzu

With the quote from Lao Tzu in mind, welcome to your first step into the world of Blockchain. Immeasurable discoveries and inventions have been made throughout Earth's history. A number of the developments are minor, some are major, some are short-lived, and other events are more critical and longer-lasting. Certain actions throughout history are so important to humanity that they are considered the major factors that led all humankind to make progress and collectively take a critical and everlasting breakthrough.

For example, consider how farming equipment and fertilizers created the exponential growth of food outputs from fixed pieces of land. Without these inventions and discoveries, the planet would not be ready to support the explosive increase we have witnessed worldwide. It was only a couple hundred years that scientists and economists indicated the top of growth, thanks to the fact that food production grew at numerical rates, doubling or tripling every certain number of years. In contrast, populations grew at exponential rates, expanding to the facility of two or more during that very same period.

Fortunately, this is often precisely what happens. Science was ready to deliver heavy farm equipment, fertilizers like ammonia, and other improvements so that food harvests could continue with the increased rates. This allowed more people to be sustained within the same land area. Without these developments, the planet would be in a completely different state.

Similarly, the invention of antibiotics, penicillin, the introduction of aviation, ocean freight, and so the heat engine, and additional recently, the sharing of information in the fashionable era with the invention of transistors and microchips have all modified the world irreversibly. As a result of these breakthroughs and innovations, we tend to have more accessible and cheaper access to merchandise and services than ever before.

When it involves the knowledge age, things have progressed at breakneck speed since the primary dot-com wave within the early to mid-90s—everything from the technologies and interface tools that have outlined how we interface and interact with technology. Everything from banking solutions to payment solutions has significantly changed over the last 50 years.

An analogous thing can be said about the first email and social networks, alongside the advancements in AI (AI) and significant data analysis, both of which have an impression on everything from helping with an online search to governance. Cooperatively, we've gone from necessary solutions for all of the above to sophisticated software services that combine various aspects of technology to deliver practical, robust, value-added, and seamless services to billions of individuals worldwide.

Yet, with all the progress comes new challenges. Therefore, the ubiquity of technology all around has begun to pose serious ethical questions and technological challenges, AI, big data, and consequently, the ability of governments to implement mass surveillance initiatives. This results in the question, where does one draw the road between illegal and legal surveillance? How can society as a whole trust the information usage collection and manipulation practices of companies and governments once they are not transparent? Where is the world headed when it involves the role of state and large corporations and their relationships with private users?

It is with this challenging and exciting background in mind that blockchain is going to be discussed. In recent years, blockchain has become a well-liked technology far more than the newest tech fad. It is a subsequent giant leap for humanity in the opinion of the many discipline experts and tech gurus. Blockchain will significantly impact our youngsters and us because the past farming and healthcare developments impacted our great-great-grandparents quite a century ago. We have now entered the new modern era.

Chapter 1 – A History of Currency, Cryptocurrency, and Blockchain

The concept behind creating a permanent, decentralized ledger, like a blockchain, was first discussed in 1991. However, the primary actual blockchain implementation was designed in 2008 by Satoshi Nakamoto (Chen, 2021). His initial design was used because the underpinning technology that runs the digital currency is referred to as bitcoin. The blockchain Mr. Satoshi engineered is the general public ledger for all bitcoin transactions. Bitcoin is a digital currency now worth roughly $22,850.80, running on blockchain technology. The foremost well-known blockchain on the market today is Bitcoin, with the Ethereum blockchain coming a close second. The technology that permits bitcoin to function as a digital currency, a useful store, and a method of exchange is blockchain because bitcoin transactions are recorded during a blockchain ledge. This suggests blockchains are not limited to running bitcoin; blockchain applications can span the whole range of finance, legal operations, trade, online exchanges, healthcare, gaming, records management, probability, and more.

Before understanding blockchain technology, you need to know how it fits our current digital currencies.

Money

Money is almost as old as humanity. Many books are written on the topic. One that is worth discovering if you are curious about the matter is the Ascent of Money: A Financial History of the planet by Niall Ferguson. Money, to work, has got to be both a store useful and a way of exchange. In the past, we've used various items for money, including gold, silver, cattle, beads, and salt. Regardless of the shape, it takes, money has got to execute these two essential functions. Also, there has got to be trust that the cash often fulfills these roles.

Cryptocurrency

A cryptocurrency is a kind of currency that has become popular over the last several years. Cryptocurrency is made using the encryption techniques of computing and arithmetic (Bashir, Mastering Blockchain: A deep dive into distributed ledgers, consensus protocols, smart contracts, DApps, cryptocurrencies, Ethereum, and more, 3rd Edition, 2020). These methods allow us to transfer funds and verify that the transfer was successful. Another crucial characteristic of cryptocurrency is that governments and central banks do not control it, making them decentralized.

These days, many of the larger banks are getting increasingly involved in evaluating the technology that creates the foundation of cryptocurrency. However, it is essential to know that any currency that arises from their endeavors will not be a true cryptocurrency because the banks control it. The foremost reliable and most dedicated cryptocurrency advocates are determined that it will not be centralized.

How Did Cryptocurrencies Develop?

Bitcoin is the greatest well-known cryptocurrency in the world today. It has been the subject of hype, fame, and publicity. The general public has been captivated by its astonishing increase in value over the last several years. They have been impressed by the tales of serious wealth that has been generated with bitcoin for those that acquired it in its infancy.

Despite its newness, people quickly realize that bitcoin is a legitimate currency. Additionally to bitcoin, many other cryptocurrencies, like bitcoin, have had massive increases in their dollar value. Legitimate governments and businesses are pursuing an increasing involvement in cryptocurrency. Despite critics, the marketplace for these currencies is flourishing. Fiat Currencies (dollar, yen, euro, and renminbi), Stocks Fiat, and Cryptocurrencies are the currencies we use daily. Despite having the word currency within the word cryptocurrency, they are more like stocks and shares of the stock exchange than fiat currencies. Once you purchase cryptocurrency, you get a number of the coins of that cryptocurrency, which acts as sort of a technology stock and a digital entry into a ledger, referred to as a blockchain.

Predecessors to Blockchain

Before the arrival of what is known as Blockchain and Bitcoin, several other projects laid the foundation for these technologies.

DigiCash

DigiCash Inc. is an electronic cash company founded in 1989 by David Sham. In 1990, David Chaum founded DigiCash to create a cashless banking software. David Chaum stated in an interview in 1999 that DigiCash Inc.s project and its technological systems entered the market before electronic commerce was fully integrated into the Internet. David Chaum was especially interested in developing systems allowing individuals conducting online transactions to have anonymity. David Chaum, the computer scientist who had already proposed the core ideas of encrypted messaging tools and is generally thought to be the father of electronic cash, proposed the entire idea in his 1982 paper, Blind signatures for untraceable payments. Use was first proposed by David Chaum, a cypherpunk dedicated to creating anonymous electronic cash.

While DigiCash did not really survive, DigiCash was a part of the foundation for the digital money that exists today. It wanted to make electronic payments anonymous, but it sadly went bust before that could fully materialize. DigiCash was designed to provide users with an alternative means of paying securely for goods and services online, itself only a few years old.

HashCash

Hashcash was proposed in 1997 by Adam Back and described in more formal terms in Back's 2002 paper Hashcash--A Countermeasure for Denial-of-Service. Bitcoin uses the Hashcash concept to ensure protection against malicious changes to the Blockchain, imposing a cost of changes which a miner should hopefully recover from rewards given for cooperating. Bitcoin uses a proof-of-work Hashcash function as its core to mining bitcoin. It was initially designed to prevent spam emails since it required a cryptographic puzzle, or a proof-of-work, to send the email. The fabled Hashcash was an email anti-spam plug-in that would generate a unique, once-useable email signature using the Proof-of-Work algorithm.

Hashcash used a proof-of-work algorithm to help create and distribute new coins, similar to many modern-day cryptocurrencies. Many elements from the

Hashcashs system have also found their way into Bitcoins development.

B-Money

Wei Dai, a well-known crypto punk, proposed B-Money in 1998 as an alternative solution to P2P banking markets that allow Internet commerce better than traditional banks controlled by authorities and managed by sector administrators. In 1998, the prolific cypherpunk Wei Dai proposed B-money, an alternate P2P, or peer-to-peer, a financial system for conducting internet commerce outside the traditional financial system controlled by corporate gatekeepers and regulated by governments.

Dais B-money proposal was never implemented in any form; however, it was striking how similar to Bitcoin (BTC) it was, especially in its use of the shared ledger and its PoW-based digital money. Although Dai's proposal for B-money was never implemented in any way, it is notable just how similar it was to the cryptocurrency, especially with the use of its blockchain network and PoW-based virtual currency.

E-Gold

Former cancer doctor Douglas Jackson was the maverick founder of e-gold, a digital first-of-its-kind that was used once by millions in over one hundred countries. Dr. Douglas Jackson made history as an early pioneer in the digital currency area when he founded E-Gold, a digital currency backed by gold, in 1996. In the mid-1990s, shortly before the advent of PayPal and over a decade before Bitcoin, a cancer doctor in Florida named Douglas Jackson Florida created a system whereby individuals could send one another digital payment tokens backed by gold. The E-gold story began in 1995 when former oncologist Douglas Jackson was still treating cancer patients.

Jackson created a system in which anybody with Internet access could redeem ownership of the digital tokens 100% for, and be redeemable for, physical gold (or, later, the physical gold equivalent of its cash value,

Or), which he would receive as collateral from clients, or purchase in regular global gold markets, and keep stored at his office. To carry out his mission for several decades, Jackson and his partner, Roger Bass, a former exec at Intuit, are developing a 2.0-era electronic gold firm called Global Standard, which, like its predecessor, will offer digital money backed by physical gold.

Douglas Jackson, Barry Downey, and Reed Jackson, as part of e-gold Ltd, Gold & Silver Reserve, Inc, filed a petition for writ of certiorari on July 2, 2020, in the U.S. District Court for the District of Columbia, pursuing a stay, without prejudice, of their 2008 convictions. On July 2, 2020, e-gold Ltd, Gold & Silver Reserve, Inc, Douglas Jackson, Barry Downey, and Reid Jackson filed a writ of Coram Nobis petition in the United States District Court for the District of Columbia, seeking to vacate, with prejudice, their 2008 convictions. Individually was charged with one count of conspiring to commit money laundering, one count of conspiring to engage in unlicensed money transmission, one count of operating an unlicensed money transmission business in violation of Federal law, and one count of operating a money transmission business without a license under D.C. E-Gold was charged in 2008 with the unlawful transmission of monetary instruments, adding the charge of laundering, and ultimately agreed to a plea deal.

Bitgold

In 2005, while studying the history of cash, Nick Szabo identified commodity money like gold bullion bits as a robust conceptual foundation for a replacement currency of the web. This new money had to be digital, scarce, incredibly costly to forge, and could not rely on trusted third parties to secure it and provide value — a digital gold, in a sense. His proposal: Bit Gold.

Bit Gold works similarly to Hashcash and particularly B-money; therein, it uses an accumulating chain of hash-based proofs-of-work periodically timestamped and published to a network of servers. The issuance and ownership of Bit Gold are recorded on a distributed property title registry — basically, a protocol that permits the governance of certain classes of property employing a quorum-based electoral system.

Where Bit Gold fell short as a currency was its lack of fungibility — i.e., when each individual unit is interchangeable for a uniform unit for an equivalent value, this is often essential for any viable sort of currency. Because the value of a touch Gold is said to be the computational cost of the proof-of-work at a selected moment in time, and since the value of computation would decrease with better machines, a unit of Bit Gold mined in 2015 would be worth, but a unit of Bit Gold mined in 2005.

Szabo proposed a second-layer solution involving a secure, trusted, auditable bank that would track the issuance of Bit Gold over time, continuously packaging the proof-of-work tokens into equal units useful, creating a stable medium of exchange. However, the system would be vulnerable to Sybil attacks that would cause a split within the network. Szabo believed any potential network split might be fixed with the honest participants continuing on their own system, which the users would naturally side with them through social consensus.

Szabo was gearing up to finally implement Bit Gold shortly before Satoshi published the planning for Bitcoin in 2008. After Bitcoin launched, he ditched the Bit Gold project, believing that Bitcoin cleverly solved the shortcomings of Bit Gold and prior digital cash experiments by synthesizing prior attempts into a system that simply worked.

Blockchains

Blockchains are digital ledgers and may be officially defined as a continuously-growing list of records that are chained together and secured using advanced cryptography (Bashir, Mastering Blockchain: A deep dive into distributed ledgers, consensus protocols, smart contracts, DApps, cryptocurrencies, Ethereum, and more, 3rd Edition, 2020).

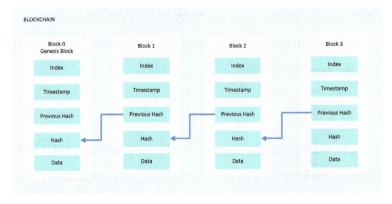

Figure 1- Diagram of a Blockchain

In additional simple terms, a blockchain is literally a sequence of blocks. Each record within a blockchain's chain's list is named a block containing specific types and pieces of data. Each block will usually include some kind of pointer as a link to the previous block, transaction data, and a time-stamp, which may take several forms. An alternative way to look at it is that a blockchain is sort of a database where every entry is linked to the previous and next entry. This suggests that the knowledge of the blockchain cannot be changed once a block with specific data is added to the chain. Counting on the chain you are looking at, there are often useful tools for exploring that will allow you to scan the transaction data. Blockchains are immune to being modified due to their inherent design. This enables blockchains to record transactions between different parties efficiently. These transactions are not only verifiable but also permanent. Once information is recorded during a blockchain, the data can not be altered after the fact without altering the next blocks by having the bulk nodes on the network agree to the change. This inability to vary the information within a blockchain makes illegal or unfair actions almost impossible to hold out. If a hacker wishes to change information within a blockchain, they might need to gain control of each node. This security is one of the foremost helpful characteristics of the blockchain.

Since blockchains are created to be immutable and verifiable, they are appropriate for drawing up agreements, documenting events, fundraising, maintaining medical records, and keeping track of other documents.

Chapter 2 - Blockchain Basics

You conduct business on a daily bases, whether or not you are aware of it. At some point, everyone goes online and initiates some kind of transaction. Whether purchasing something from Amazon or buying something from iTunes, you are engaging within the blockchain technology business.

Even though the term "blockchain" is comparatively new, the technology has been around for a few decades. The digitized ledger that Satoshi Nakamoto created in 2008 was the idea for the spreadsheets that manage cryptocurrencies and other online trading transactions. The technology is employed in cryptography, which is how text is coded on the web.

Cryptography is employed in blockchain technology to make distributed trust networks. This allows any contributor to the system to work the transactions securely without getting authorization from somebody else within the digital ledger. These transactions are verified, approved, and recorded in an encrypted block.

This block is saved from time to time and then connected to the previous block, which successively creates a sequence.

Components of a Blockchain

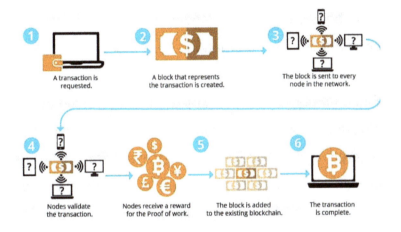

Figure 2 - How Blockchain works

Two main parts structure a blockchain. The primary component is the decentralized network. The decentralized network is what enables and verifies the transactions that are made. Having blockchains on a decentralized network means the software is not limited to at least one computing system. Instead, it is often controlled by multiple computer systems, and more importantly, it is not controlled by the government.

The second component is the entire ledger, where the transactions are processed and recorded in a secure location. This security makes it almost impossible for somebody who is not connected to the chain to form changes or steal information.

Since numerous contributors are often involved in any blockchain, any contributors can control the knowledge entered into the ledger. Since every transaction is processed securely and given a permanent time-stamp, it can become challenging for an additional contributor to change the ledger.

Blockchain technology is often used for various computerized and internet-based applications. One among these applications is smart- contracts. Smart contracts allow businesses to verify and execute independent agreements in a secure environment. Blockchain technology acts as an intermediary for implementing all business deals, protocols, and programmed data exchanges in smart contracts. As more and more transactions are completed online to run our personal and professional lives, more and more deals are being signed and created online.

Blockchain applications have become increasingly popular in the medical field in recent years. Researchers are now investigating these applications handling digital identity, insurance records, and medical records. Many medical offices today use some digital machine to verify that the knowledge they need on file is, in fact, your information.

Security Concerns

One of the foremost significant issues people are faced with today is the thought that each one their information might be compromised by hackers because most of our personal information is digitized. It also seems that It is becoming too easy for complete strangers to access, copy and tamper with data. However, It is still a threat that we all take regardless of the increased probability of being hacked. Blockchain technology was created to ensure that does not happen or at the very least make it harder to undertake.

For someone to hack the blockchain system, they might have to return and alter every block. That might require much effort and patience because blockchains could have upwards of billions of chains linked that an individual would need to undergo and alter. Changing only one or two blocks would automatically send an alert that the system is being hacked. This is often just one of the various reasons why blockchain technology has become so popular.

Blockchain technology is often used for the spread of other data also. It also can be used for global payments, sharing music, or tracking diamond sales.

Types of Blockchain
There are three major sorts of blockchain. There are:

1. Private blockchains

2. Public blockchains
3. Consortium blockchains

The general public creates public blockchains. Anyone can participate in creating, confirming, and recording the content that is put into the blockchain. There is not only one person responsible for overseeing the transactions during this blockchain.

Because there is not one person responsible for those blockchains, decisions are made by many decentralized agreement tools like proof of labor, a computer algorithm employed by cryptocurrencies like bitcoin. Public blockchains are open and clear in content, making it easy for anyone who looks at them to know what they are and what they will do.

On the other hand, public blockchains are privately owned by a private person or organization. With public blockchains, there is one designated person responsible. While there are often several contributors to the present sort of blockchain, the ultimate transactions are either approved or disapproved by the person responsible and then recorded.

The purpose of consortium blockchains, also referred to as federated blockchains, is to eliminate the sole autonomy given to only one contributor by utilizing personal blockchains. This sort of blockchain allows for quite one contributor to be responsible. Instead, there's a gaggle of companies or individuals that gather and make decisions that benefit the whole network.

Blockchain Technology Overview

Blockchain technology is an encrypted, irreversible, decentralized ledger that has the capability to form all centralized activities, processes, and organizations entirely autonomous. This suggests that an individual will have the power to eliminate the middleman and specialists, effectively reforming every business worldwide.

Blockchain technology is simply how to stay track of any money or trading exchanges you engage in online.

You will consider it like an accountant who keeps track of all the cash that you spend. Currently, blockchain technology is usually wont to handle any situation dealing with cryptocurrency, like bitcoin. Let's consider the subsequent example.

When you complete a bitcoin transaction, that specific transaction is processed through the blockchain. Before the transaction is often achieved, you or someone connected to your bitcoin account has to verify that the transaction is legitimate. Once the transaction is often confirmed as valid, it is recorded and saved to a ledger controlled by the blockchain. As of now, nobody can change or alter the transaction in any way. Only you or those with access to your account can verify transactions.

Blockchain technology is controlled by a decentralized network, which suggests that any government does not control it. By running on a decentralized system, It is much easier to conduct business transactions. It is also more private because you do not have a federal bank holding your money or other assets. You and your company strictly handle everything.

Centralization Example

When you use your open-end credit at the bookstore, you swipe your card to buy your purchases. The corporate then send a bill to your bank for the quantity agreed to once you purchase your goods. The bank then must verify that it had been you who made the acquisition. Once the transaction is confirmed, the bank releases the funds to the corporate and records the transaction in their ledger. The bank documented the transaction in the ledger, including all the operations the bank made on behalf of the credit card you used. The bank has total control over what happens with the ledger. Aside from having the power to look at your banking statements, you've no authority to vary anything or do anything with the ledger. Centralized ledgers are much simpler to hack because multiple entities control them.

Decentralized Example

Imagine that you simply want to transfer 1.00 bitcoin to someone. All you've got to do is tell whoever is responsible for the network, whether It is one person or a gaggle of individuals, that you simply are transferring 1.00 bitcoin. After this, the transaction is approved and recorded.

Decentralized blockchains are far better than centralized transactions because it takes less time to finish one transaction. Another reason decentralized blockchains are better is that an individual or company can send secure information to a different person or company, such as encrypted messages and medical records (Bashir, Mastering Blockchain Second Edition, 2018).

Chapter 3 - The Business of Blockchain

Each person has trust concerns with something in their lives. Many of us today do not trust inputting their information into the web. However, even with this mistrust, it has not stopped many of us from continuing to try to do it.

One purpose of blockchain technology is to ease people's distrust in inputting their information on the web. It is one of the biggest reasons companies are increasingly investing their funds in using this technology. A study showed that, between 2013 and 2022, blockchain-managed funds reached a total of $50 billion (Statista Research Department, 2022).

Different Industries that Use Blockchain Technology

The financial industry is among the sectors that have greatly benefitted from utilizing blockchain technology. This is often due to the vast sums of cash and transactions that are live within the industry. Here are a few examples of several companies utilizing blockchain technology today (Roy, 2020).

• *Crowdlending*

Crowdlending campaigns have begun to take over the act of getting to travel to the bank to urge a loan. Crowdlending may be a person-to-person lending company. Today, on average, 50 billion person-to-person loans are being made worldwide. This industry will likely feel a huge boost with the utilization of blockchain technology.

• *IBM Global Financing Unit*

IBM has become one of the main players in blockchain technology use, with a proven diary of being an excellent resource for tracing transactions. IBM's Global Financing Unit processes $2.9 million in payables for the corporate per annum. It is also liable for granting credit to quite four thousand suppliers. IBM has successfully lowered dispute settlements by 25 percent, thanks partially to blockchain technology. This decrease in percentage has resulted in the group having the ability to release $100 million in pre-confirmed capital for other purposes.

• ***Bookkeeping***

The bookkeeping industry has greatly benefited from blockchain technology. Every transaction that takes place within the economy today is registered internally within the private records of individual market participants. Blockchain technology takes place when accounting expands past the borders of the network.

Adding Value to Your Business

There are numerous ways in which blockchain technology can add value to a business. A method is by building a network for your business. Dr. Michael Yuan, the Chief Scientist of CyberMiles, notes how blockchain can provide value to startups and corporations. His theory is that the key advantage of blockchains will deliver the power to construct a network for all types of businesses. His theory states that instead of competing against one another, companies can cooperate and develop a system with every business industry having its own chain (Jai Singh Arun, 2019).

Another way that blockchain technology can add value to a business is by banking the unbanked. It'd be hard to believe, but there are tons of individuals within the world who do not have bank accounts. Blockchain technology will allow these people to make a checking account. Someone could just open a bitcoin account and reciprocally have a digital wallet.

A third way in which blockchain technology can increase the value of a business is by reducing the time for transactions to be complete. Again, time is playing a big role within the blockchain world. Christopher Brown, CEO of Modular, create Blossom, a digital wallet for Ethereum. The program may be a multi-featured desktop wallet application that gives businesses and users a more straightforward thanks for handling their funds. It takes a smaller amount of time than if you were to go to the bank to urge cash.

Next, blockchain technology can add value to businesses through legal contracts. This will be done by linking the web of Things (IoT) data and blockchain technology. Utilizing the information from IoT devices allows individuals and businesses to attach to legal contracts that are saved on the blockchain. For instance, once you buy a house, all the documents you simply sign must be signed by the vendor. This suggests that each one of the documents must be in one place for both parties to possess access. Outside information from IoT-connected devices is linked to the blockchain, making the legal contracts immediately usable without anyone having the ability to interfere with the process (Dr. Seok-Won Lee, 2021).

The final way that blockchain technology can increase the value of a business is by assisting with monetization. The ways companies are making profits are changing. People do not concentrate on ads because you now fast-forward through the commercials and online. Plus, the cash generally goes to the ad's location, significantly impacting business (Shelper, 2019).

Blockchain technology solves this problem. This is regularly because every part of the content created for ads is logged on the blockchain, which is how content creators are compensated through fiat currency or cryptocurrency.

Growing Money

Many experts think that blockchain technology will become the way of the future. Cryptocurrency is rapidly growing because people want to place their money in a place that is not only safe and secure but which will also gain value sort of a bank account. However, savings accounts are not as secure as they would like.

By the top of 2017, future markets had already been designed for bitcoin. That was also the year the finance industry saw a dramatic increase in Initial Coin Offerings, (ICO). Over the last year, ICOs have gained more money than risk capital investments.

While cryptocurrencies still improve in their abilities to process transactions quickly, eventually, they will compete against MasterCard companies processing transactions.

The Cloud and Blockchain

At some point, everyone has used the cloud to copy data that they wish to save. If you did not know, the cloud actually runs on a blockchain. Experts say that we have begun to take luxury without any consideration. In the past, you could not merely click a button and automatically save data to a backup site like iCloud or OneDrive.

Instead, you were required to transfer the knowledge on a compact disc or flash drive. Then, you'd need to take the disk or flash drive to a different computer to download the information.

While you will still do that today, there's no guarantee that this technology will last. Just like the floppy disks of the past, compact discs and flash drives may become obsolete, but internet-saving applications will always be updated because we now live in a tech-savvy world.

Blockchain and Gaming

eSports and online fantasy sports have grown significantly over the last decade, with more and more people creating online fantasy sports teams. Online games, like Fantasy Football, were a number of the primary sites to embrace the earliest versions of bitcoin and other cryptocurrencies. They also use blockchain technology to operate and continue with the gaming technology.

The uses of blockchain technology do not just stop with fantasy sports. The foremost popular smartphone applications to download today are games. This is often why, as the technology grows, more developers will likely make use of blockchains, also as cryptocurrencies.

Supply Chain Management and Blockchain

Blockchain technology can also improve supply chain management by providing how to trace goods at an equivalent nonce cost-effective—for instance, sending packages through United Parcel Services from one business to a different. In the past, someone had to call to find out where their package was if it had not arrived when it had been alleged to. Today, you are given a tracking number that permits you to ascertain where the package you sent or are expecting is in transit, which creates a blockchain.

Blockchain technology has made it easier for businesses to do business together because it dramatically simplified the assembly and transfer process and the verification and payment methods used.

Blockchain Technology and Quality Assurance

In business, mistakes happen, regardless of how careful you are and how closely you follow processes and procedures. It is often challenging to pin down how the error occurred. With blockchain technology, mistakes and errors are often traced back to their origin. Not only does this make it simpler to research mistakes, but it also saves companies time and money.

Chapter 4 - Blockchain Career Opportunities

Blockchain Career Opportunities – what proportion does one get purchased having Blockchain expertise? As Blockchain is considered together with the fastest-developing skill sets, the number of jobs is growing at an interesting rate. As a result, Blockchain professionals' salaries are higher compared to other IT professionals. The Blockchain talent pool is sort of limited still. Despite the same fact that there are many high-paying jobs, people with blockchain skill sets are hard to seek out. This is often why big tech giants like Amazon, Facebook, and Microsoft have their own teams to review and research blockchain spaces (Weston, 2022).

The demand for blockchain professionals is there in almost every sector, just like the BFSI sector (banking, financial services, and insurance), supply chain healthcare, gaming, real estate et al. . Even some government organizations have also applied blockchain technology in their operations.

On average, the salary of a blockchain developer at the junior level might be around $120,748 within the US. However, with a fair amount of skills and expertise, one can earn over $150k yearly within the US. The higher the experience and the higher your skillset is, the higher are going to be the yearly compensation. Also, the salary range varies, counting on what degree you have got and in what position you are working.

Blockchain Career Options

Blockchain has been ready to revolutionize both massive corporations and start-ups. So you will find a blockchain job in many areas and industries.

Let's take a glance at the career options within the blockchain space:

Blockchain Developer
Blockchain developers work as full-stack developers. This career might be an honest option if one has great expertise in server-side programming and excellent analytical skills. With an understanding of fixing nodes,

the top to finish systems of blockchain applications, the way to submit these transactions, the way to proceed with blockchain transactions, and the way to trigger Smart Contract functions can assist you in landing employment. Skills like:

AJAX	C++
Microsoft SQL Server	REST
NET	FTP
Visual Studio	HTML
SQL	XML
JavaScript	MYSQL
C	

These skills can be used to gain employment as a blockchain developer. Several hospitable industries hire a blockchain developer, which incorporates financial services, government departments, and tech companies.

Blockchain Quality Engineer

A blockchain quality engineer is liable for taking care of all the areas of quality within the development process, including automation framework testing and manual testing, conducting research, devising a strategy for load performance tests, and advising on blockchain tools. This profession entails dealing in planning, QA, and delivery of intricate blockchain projects. They are also accountable for ensuring that each QA standard is maintained. Someone with both engineering and MBA degrees is often a great candidate for this role.

Blockchain Legal Consultants

As blockchain technology falls under more supervisory inspection, companies and organizations implementing the technology got to appoint or contract legal counsel within the initial stages. Thus, blockchain legal consulting may be a good career option. People having a considerable understanding of the method of blockchain from development to implementation can choose a career as a blockchain legal consultant. They need to know the arrangement and how to administer the process and guide the businesses accordingly. Legal partnerships and contracts associated with blockchain also are what a blockchain legal consultant must oversee. As a legal consultant following tasks can also need to be performed:

- Drafting legal agreements
- Performing due diligence

Blockchain Designers

To be a blockchain designer, one must be proficient in – PS, Illustrator, UI designs (web and mobile), etc. Good communication skills would even be a severe benefit to this career.

Blockchain Project Manager

Companies must contact blockchain project managers to seek blockchain solutions for successful blockchain projects in any organization. They are liable for both the success and failure of the project. Blockchain project managers are employed to supervise, plan, and implement projects to understand the specific goals of the businesses. In straightforward terms, they are required to manage and facilitate blockchain projects.

Blockchain programmer

A blockchain programmer may be a programming expert with education and training in software design and computing. To be a blockchain programmer, one would require a practical knowledge of cloud technologies and management.

Blockchain Product Manager

For those with a decent amount of programming knowledge, the work of a blockchain product manager is often a great career option. A blockchain product manager is used to seem after the event, coding, and distribution roles. A blockchain product manager's two most vital duties are to steer time-sensitive projects and regulate the event budget.

Risk Analyst

Together with the best paying blockchain jobs worldwide, Risk analysts are liable for evaluating risks, supporting programming, information analytics, product improvement, and project documentation.

Business Analyst

This job involves examining the viability of innovations and projects. The job of a business analyst is to gauge technologies. They work to seek out what products would attract the audience. They also use their analytical, coding, and statistical know-how to help effective customer-centric services.

Crypto Community Manager

Crypto Community Manager plays a crucial role in marketing and client interactions. As network administrators, they track and present engagement statistics and overall marketing.

Blockchain jobs in Banking

the utilization of blockchain technology in banking has increased, giving rise to career opportunities for blockchain experts to possess a career within the banking sector. Blockchain technology in the financial sector is so widespread because it improves efficiency, enhances security, offers unchangeable records, provides quick transaction time, prevents third-party involvement, and reduces costs. With the utilization of blockchain technology in banking, payment solutions and KYC and Document verification process has become very efficient and smooth.

Example job descriptions

Senior Blockchain Engineering Manager

Senior leader to oversee and manage the development efforts of our Marketplace for primary offerings and alternative trading system (ATS) / exchange for the secondary trading of digital asset securities. This individual will liaise with numerous technology solution providers and partners to ensure that our Marketplace and ATS technically perform as intended and align with our compliance and regulatory requirements.

Responsibilities for this role include, but are not limited to the following:

- Lead, supervise and mentor the development teams responsible for creating the Marketplace and ATS.

- Assess and choose the blockchain technology solutions and partners that best suit the organization and align with the company's vision (digital wallet providers, custodians, transfer agents, etc.).
- Work closely with the Product and Marketing teams to ensure that we leverage efficient and performant blockchain technology/infrastructure solutions to properly conduct our day-to-day operations and deliver a best-of-breed offering to our customers (blockchain protocols, automated market markets, etc.).
- Work closely with the Compliance team to ensure that we are responsible about the technology solutions we choose to run/grow our business while at the same time adhering to our regulatory and corporate governance requirements.
- Act as a subject matter expert on such things as the latest digital asset technology standards, including content management systems, infrastructure, hardware/software solutions, and the latest engineering practices.

Requirements for this role are as follows:

- Ability to oversee and manage our day-to-day operations, stay abreast of digital trends in the blockchain space, and understand how they impact our various lines of business.
- Demonstrate exceptional leadership and communication skills to present the case for various blockchain technologies to be acquired, sourced, updated, and decommissioned, ensuring that we leverage the most suitable tools to add maximum value to our organization while simultaneously adhering to our regulatory requirements and responsibilities.
- Capable of reviewing and assessing technology products/systems to determine their potential value to our customers and the organization.

Blockchain Solution Architect

Responsibilities: Understand business processes and define business requirements. Conceptualize and design blockchain-based solutions. As a Solution Architect developed architecture design and led the development team.

Qualifications:

- 10+ years of work experience as a solution architect
- 5+ years of experience designing and delivering solutions with one or more blockchain platforms such as R3 Corda, Hyperledger Fabric, DAML, Enterprise Ethereum, Hyperledger Indy/Aries.
- Deep understanding of the Blockchain ecosystem, concepts, and broad range of use cases across industries
- Experience in the application of blockchain in financial services is preferred
- Knowledge of blockchain solutions for digital asset custody is desirable

Blockchain Security Engineer

Requirements

- Passionate about Cryptocurrency/ Defi/ Blockchain
- +2 years of experience in Solidity, Ethereum Virtual Machine (EVM), and/or blockchain technology.
- Minimum educational background: Bachelors' degree or a Master's or Ph.D. in Computer Sciences or Security Information.
- Minimum of 3+ years professional experience as Software Engineer or Security Engineer.
- Solid experience in threat analysis, advanced persistent threat (APT), or response.
- Experienced in threat and vulnerability management, penetration testing, and SecOps (intrusion detection, security logging, malware analysis, and forensics)
- Direct experience with RUST

- Experience in programming languages such as Golang and Solidity.
- Strong background in Math, specifically formal methods, a plus

Responsibilities

- Work directly with the external blockchain developers to audit their code and secure their products, including smart contracts, protocols, and dapp.
- Contribute to our internal security tools and create new ones that help for improving the security services by following good engineering practices.
- Conduct security research and publish your findings in technical blog posts/conferences.
- Improve our processes and offering and strive for the satisfaction of our clients

Junior Blockchain Developer

Qualifications

- This position requires an individual with a commitment, drive, and passion for new technologies, staying current in emerging trends, and participating in relevant forums and events
- Must be flexible, able to work in a highly collaborative environment, juggle multiple tasks at once, and work independently and collaboratively as needed
- Superior interpersonal skills and strong communication skills are critical
- 1+ years experience with open-source application development stacks
- 1+ years experience with development on either Python or Java
- 1+ years experience leading emerging technology product development
- 1+ years experience with the Amazon Web Services platform
- 1+ years in implementing blockchain projects
- Agile development exposure
- Ability to work independently

- Excellent oral and written communication skills
- Excellent documentation skills
- Bachelor's Degree from an accredited college or university with a major in Computer Science, Information Systems, Engineering, or other related scientific or technical discipline
- Suitable experience can be used to substitute for education
- Work location is remote, but infrequent onsite meetings (post-pandemic) will be needed
- Background and financial history credit checks are necessary for obtaining a public trust clearance if assigned to one of our Government services projects

Responsibilities

- As part of this role, you will be working on multiple emerging technology initiatives for Software services and products company
- Serve as a junior developer working under our Emerging Technologies Lead
- Perform hands-on work related to blockchain, microservices, and agile tooling

- Assist team leads in identifying multiple emerging tech initiatives running in parallel related to such technologies as blockchain and agile tooling
- Perform as a hands-on junior developer to implement solutions
- Be willing to engage in developing online content (blogs, social media, etc.) specific to initiatives to further corporate marketing initiatives

Web3 / Blockchain Engineer

Qualifications

- 5+ years of Web2 experience; proficient with backend languages/ frameworks (e.g. Python, Node, JS, Flask, Django, etc.)
- Solid Web3 experience; proficient with a blockchain scripting/ smart-contract language (e.g., Solidity); has deployed projects to mainnet
- Passionate about testing code for completeness, accuracy, and security

- Experience with developing and scaling databases and micro-services/ distributed computing
- Cloud-native - Knowledge of cloud infrastructure technology (AWS, Azure, etc.)
- Experienced with writing software that speaks a variety of network protocols, with awareness of appropriate threading/locking models or asynchronous design to ensure correctness
- Ability to work within an environment of continuous integration and deployment
- Fluent English
- Excellent verbal and written communication

Responsibilities

- Develop and maintain blockchain software (including integrations, security, and testing) in a performant, high-uptime environment
- Build products based on various well-established blockchain protocols (Ethereum, Polygon, and more)

- Integrate with blockchain protocols from various backend servers, supporting the creation of APIs and integrations
- Assist in architecting cryptocurrency plans and platform selection along with wallet integrations
- Design, develop and implement key system and application architecture components that support the creation, transfer, and storage of digital assets
- Develop to highest security best practices
- Implement test-driven development; drive test automation
- Help identify product requirements and design architecture with Products and Engineering teams
- Improve test coverage of codebase

Where are you able to find a blockchain job?
If you are getting involved with the blockchain technology sector and are checking out opportunities within the US, you will start your search on job portals, where you will find the newest job postings from the blockchain industry. You will filter and search for either

entry-level or expert jobs. A useful place to start your search would be Blockchain Works blockchain.workshub.com, a fanatical blockchain jobs portal.

Blockchain Career
Some steps you will fancy start your journey into the blockchain industry are:
1. First, you will enroll yourself in some Blockchain Courses. Consequently, you will achieve a blockchain certification.
2. While browsing the course, confirm your understanding of all the essential terms within the field. Being familiar with terminology is extremely important. For better understanding, undergo various YouTube videos, as they also supply technical details and practical demonstrations.
3. Try to participate in several blockchain conferences and events. This may assist you in understanding more about the industry dynamics.

4. Focus on developing and improving programming knowledge and cryptography skills.
5. Educating yourself in smart contracts and distributed computing could even be a good idea.

Courses for Blockchain Technology: If you are hooked on learning Blockchain technology and have plans to pursue a career in blockchain, you will go for a blockchain certification course. These courses will assist you in studying relevant areas in cryptocurrency and the broader blockchain space. It will also help you to excel within the core blockchain platforms. You will get to understand about Bitcoin, how it works, and a few critical vocabulary. Specialized courses offer detailed blockchain instructions and valuable guidelines that give you a transparent perception of blockchain technology and its application.

Blockchain Career Opportunities – Conclusion

As the blockchain space continues to increase, the probability of getting hired at a blockchain company is high, with many opportunities available. Experts believe Blockchain is here to remain and will play a crucial role in both lifestyle and business. Thus, big tech giants, large banks, governments, and little startups will constantly demand Blockchain expertise and Blockchain professionals. Therefore, this is often the proper time to start brooding about a blockchain career and taking the proper steps to urge there!

Chapter 5 - Proof of labor vs. Proof of Stake

Most of the general public blockchains currently available are supported as a symbol of labor system. However, in 2018, the second biggest cryptocurrency, Ethereum, began testing a replacement system that might change its blockchain from a Proof of labor to a Proof of Stake system. Before we get into what this suggests, knowing what happens when a transaction is verified is essential (Bashir, Mastering Blockchain Second Edition, 2018).

Proof of labor

The mining of bitcoin is accomplished by employing a high-powered machine that will utilize SHA256 double round features, a verification process intending to validate bitcoin transactions. This is often done to supply security for the sanctity of the bitcoin blockchain. The speed at which your machine can mine bitcoins is measured regarding hashes per second.

In exchange for this service, Bitcoin compensates people who do the mining by offering them a fraction of a bitcoin for each validation. They are doing this to offset time and energy costs. Additionally, those that initiate the transaction will typically provide some amount of a transaction fee to assist offset costs also. The upper the pc processing power of your bitcoin mining machine, the more you will make through the method.

To be allowed into the blockchain, each block must have a legitimate proof of labor; a proof of labor may be a sort of data that is both difficult to supply and time-consuming. Creating a proof of labor is actually a random process with a probability of success. This suggests that a bitcoin mining machine trying to finish the method requires much trial and error. Bitcoin uses what's referred to as the hashcash proof of labor.

The hashcash proof of labor may be a sort of cryptographic algorithm that uses a hash function as a primary building block of the mining process. The primary standard hashcash function used today is the haschash-Sha256. This particular proof of labor function was created by Dr. Adam Back in the 1990s. It was initially used to stop email spam abuse because successfully generating the hashcash for one email was simple. However, creating one for a massive number of emails at an equivalent time proved to be far more complex.

You can tweak hashcash proofs of labor for the problem to ensure that new blocks are not being generated faster than the network can handle. This suggests that a replacement block cannot be generated once every ten minutes at this point because the probability of each consecutive generation is minimal. This makes it difficult to ascertain which bitcoin machine will get subsequent blocks.

For a replacement block to be considered valid, its hash value must end up being but that of the present target. Every block must indicate that employment has been completed to get it naturally. Each block also contains the preceding block's hash, which is how the chain understands where each block falls within the general blockchain. To vary a block, the work must be redone on all the preceding blocks, and new and connected hashes must be calculated for all of them. The blockchain is then essentially shielded from tampering due to the necessary computational power.

Proof of Stake

Many cryptocurrencies today get rid of some variation of the proof of labor model, either through the SHA256 hash or another similar hash. However, Ethereum, bitcoin's largest competitor, has been performing on an alternate that would drastically change the way blockchain transactions are verified.

In early 2017, Ethereum released the application guide for a hybrid proof of work/proof of stake system. They are rolling out this new system in phases before creating the platform's primary verification system (@wackerow, 2022). The plan at present states that the blockchain platform will alternate between the two systems. About one out of each 100 blocks will use the new system with the new one, while the remainder will still use the old one.

The hope is that the new system will improve the speed at which they will produce new blocks. This may mark the primary step within the plans for Ethereum's evolution. This may be the primary time a symbol of stake system will be what to secure a blockchain, which can be a significant breakthrough. This new system will function the proof of concept test for an alternative to the proof of labor model that dominates the cryptocurrency today and supply proponents the power to check their claim of its advantage. When the new proof of stake model is unrolled on a bigger scale, it will significantly reduce the quantity of electricity that is required to verify one block.

It is essential to know just how the proof of stake system differs from the proof of labor model. With proof of stake verification, instead of having the miner resolve the equation to verify the block, a validator, who is confirmed trustworthy by the stake they need within the system, will plan to its accuracy. They know they will also lose their own ether if they cheat.

During the primary stage of deployment, all of the blocks that are validated through the new system will also be tested through the old system to double verify that the blocks contain the knowledge they ought to while testing the accuracy of the new system. Validators will then check out the available chains and make a choice supported what proportion ether is currently within the chain. If they create a bad choice, they will lose their money. This practice will help form a consensus that results in one more massive chain from the various smaller ones.

Benefits of the Proof of Stake Model

While the method of implementing the proof of stake model is not smooth sailing, it does not suggest that the proof of stake system goes to lose out. It contains many obvious benefits over the more traditional process. The first clear benefit of this new model is that it will drop the nearly a million dollars Ethereum miners spend on electricity daily to around $100,000 or simply one-tenth.

In addition to making it inexpensive to mine cryptocurrency, the proof of stake model will also make it more unrestricted because it would not matter how fast the user's computer performs; the calculations will be completed within the blockchain. As a plus, this makes the 51 percent attack far more challenging to be successful. A 51 percent attack occurs when a group of miners joins in controlling 51 percent of all nodes running a specific blockchain to create false blocks to the system that the unaffected nodes will accept as accurate because a majority of the nodes are already reporting it that way.

Proof of stake also will make it possible to ensure the validators stay honest by forcing them to be vested in the transactions they verify because they know they will lose their own money if they do not play fair. In the end, the proof of stake model makes it simpler to supply blocks faster than ever because of the sharding process of breaking a more extensive database down into more manageable pieces. When databases are weakened, each bit can possess its own set of validators who complete their own transactions within the shard. Once this happens, it makes scalability more modular and even faster.

Proof of Stake Challenges

The new process would not be without its own share of issues. The primary issue will be that the new system is not bound to work. This is often because this sort of model hasn't been put into play at an outsized scale before. This suggests that there's an opportunity that the first blockchain might be damaged if the transactions are not processed as planned or if a smart contract is miswritten. To prevent this scenario, the Ethereum team is functioning on what's called the finality property. This may ensure that the present state of the blockchain will be secure before the new one is often implemented.

Chapter 6 - Benefits of Blockchain Technology

The potential of blockchain technology saw all of the world's contracts and agreements digitized into code and stored publicly, transparent databases that are safe from being deleted, tampered with, or revised. The longer term will see all kinds of agreements, business processes, online tasks, funds payments, and transactions with one digital record, which will be identified and validated; because the technology continues to expand, we'll see middlemen, like lawyers, stock market brokers, and banks, saving billions, if not trillions of dollars per annum (Blockchain - Benefits, Drawbacks and Everything You Need to Know, n.d.).

Blockchain technology is perfectly suited to revolutionizing the way many industries do business. Here are just a few of the ways in which blockchain technology will achieve this.

Eliminating Third Parties

Blockchain technology will eliminate third parties and increase the number of exchanges that are not subject to trust issues.

Blockchain will allow two or more parties to conduct a transaction, of any type, without having to resort to official oversight or intermediation with an external party. This may significantly reduce or maybe eliminate counterparty risks.

Counterparty risk may be a risk that every contract party will face if the counterparty does not meet their contractual obligations. It is a risk to both parties and is something that should always be considered when evaluating a contract.

Control Over Data

With blockchain, users are more empowered and have better control over their own data. With blockchain protocols in place, users own and are on top of all their information and transactions themselves. Uber may be a great example of this. Uber is one of the world's leading car services companies, but they do not own any of the cars that operate its business; they earn billions of dollars through car rides that are logged by drivers using the Uber app.

Better Data Quality and Integrity

With blockchain technology, data is usually complete because a subsequent block cannot be generated or mined without being chained to a verified block being finished within the chain. It is also consistent because all the information has got to conform to the protocol standards; alternatively, it would not be recorded within the chain and is commonly available.

Durability and Reliability

Blockchain technology has been recognized not to have one point of failure and can withstand malicious exterior attacks more efficiently. This is often compared to closed systems with possible weaknesses and points of failure scattered throughout the whole system.

The Integrity of knowledge Processing and Transfers

Due to the immutable nature of the blocks in a blockchain, every user on the network can trust that each transaction they create will happen on the network. They will always be executed precisely because the system was designed. This eliminates the need for any third party to oversee the transactions, maintaining the integrity of the information being processed and everyone transfers.

Transparency and Auditability

All transactions made to and on a blockchain are, by design, created on a public ledger which everyone will check out. This creates a highly transparent system that anyone will search. Various services, like etherscan, permit users to look at the vast databases and transactions to audit everything happening within and on a blockchain.

Faster Transactions

Like ACH (automated clearinghouse transactions), bank transactions can take days to clear. This is often true for transactions made outside of regular working hours. Just believe once you send a wire or make a sale at the top of the business day on Friday. Without blockchains, you cannot ascertain any timely updates to the status of your funds. Often you are not provided with an update until the subsequent Tuesday or Wednesday. Blockchain technology decreases the transaction times to minutes and sometimes even seconds, which are processed round the clock.

Lower Transaction Costs

With blockchains, no outside parties are overlooking the transactions; due to this, blockchains can potentially reduce transaction fees significantly. This reduction in transaction fees could save billions of dollars annually.

Chapter 7 - Decentralized Finance (DeFi)

Decentralized finance (DeFi) is an economic system that runs on a decentralized network of computers instead of one server. DeFi is an evolving digital financial infrastructure that theoretically eliminates the necessity for a financial institution or agency to approve financial transactions. Regarded by many as an umbrella term for a replacement wave of monetary services innovation, DeFi is deeply connected with blockchain -- the decentralized, immutable, public ledger on which Bitcoin is predicated -- that permits all computers (or nodes) on a network to carry a replica of the history of transactions. The thought is that no single entity has control over, or can alter, that ledger of transactions (Harvey, 2021).

Most of the financial services defined as DeFi are often found on the Ethereum network, the second-largest cryptocurrency marketplace, which also acts as a platform that permits other blockchain apps to be built thereon (Ethereum's cryptocurrency, Ether, is employed to pay transaction costs). By utilizing decentralized apps, or dApps, two or more parties can exchange, lend, borrow, and trade directly using blockchain technology and smart contracts without intermediaries' involvement and costs.

How is DeFi different from Bitcoin?

While Bitcoin may be a decentralized digital currency that operates on its own blockchain and is employed mostly as a store useful, DeFi may be a concept that describes financial services that are made on public blockchains, like Bitcoin and Ethereum, that, for instance, enable users to earn interest or borrow against their cryptocurrency holdings. DeFi comprises various applications for financial services like trading, borrowing, lending, and derivatives.

How does DeFi work?

DeFi uses cryptocurrencies and smart contracts to supply financial services to eliminate the necessity for intermediaries like guarantors. Such services include lending (where users can lend out their cryptocurrency and earn interest in minutes instead of once a month), receiving a loan instantly, making peer-to-peer trades without a broker, saving cryptocurrency, and earning a far better rate of interest than from a bank, and buying derivatives like stock options and futures contracts.

To facilitate peer-to-peer business transactions, users utilize dApps, most of which may be found on the Ethereum network, as well as the additional widely used DeFi services and dApps are coins (Ether, Polkadot, Solana), digital wallets (Coinbase, MetaMask), stablecoins (whose value is pegged to a currency like the US Dollar), tokens DeFi mining (liquidity mining), yield farming, trading, staking, borrowing, lending, and saving using smart contracts.

DeFi is open source, meaning that protocols and apps are theoretically open for users to examine and innovate upon. As a result, users can mix and match protocols to unlock unique combinations of opportunities by developing their own dApps.

What is a smart contract?

It is code that acts as a digital agreement between two parties. A smart contract that runs on a blockchain is stored on a public database and cannot be altered. Because the blockchain processes smart contracts, they will be sent automatically without a 3rd party. The peer-to-peer transaction is closed only if the conditions within the agreement are met (Marcelo Corrales Compagnucci, 2021).

The apparent advantage of smart contracts is that they will be created for you to borrow and lend your cryptocurrency without using an intermediary, which sidesteps tons of the risks involved in traditional lending. If, for instance, a borrower can not meet their obligations during a loan, their lender can simply take their funds back, making the necessity for collateral unnecessary. Moreover, DeFi saving accounts could function the same way as savings accounts at banks but might offer higher interest rates or disburse daily, weekly, or monthly, counting on the platform.

Who created DeFi?

No one person created the concept of decentralized finance. Bitcoin is claimed to have been created by Satoshi Nakamoto, a pseudonym for an individual, or a group of people, behind the world's first cryptocurrency and financial blockchain. Truth identity, or identities behind Satoshi Nakamoto, remain unknown.

Ethereum, the platform inspired by Bitcoin, and therefore the one on which a majority of DeFi services run, was developed by programmer-turned-entrepreneur Vitalik Buterin. In 2013, at the age of 19, the Russian-Canadian wrote a white book outlining an alternate platform to Bitcoin that might enable programmers to develop their own apps employing a built-in programing language. Thus, Ethereum was born, and It is grown exponentially over the past nine years. As of mid-January 2022, the market cap for Ethereum's cryptocurrency, Ether, is $385 billion. It is the second-largest cryptocurrency by market cap behind Bitcoin, which still reigns because the biggest cryptocurrency with a market cap valued at $431 billion, consistent with CoinMarketCap.

What are you able to do with DeFi?

As mentioned above, DeFi uses cryptocurrencies and smart contracts to supply financial services without the involvement of banks. With the addition of more dApps, the chances of what you will do with DeFi still grow. The more common uses of DeFi include sending funds anywhere within the world (in little time and affordably); storing money using crypto wallets (and earning higher yields than at a standard bank); lending and borrowing on a peer-to-peer level; trading cryptocurrencies anonymously and at any time 24/7; trade tokenized versions of investments like stocks, funds, other financial assets and non-fungible tokens (NFTs); crowdfunding; and buying insurance with the assistance of companies like Etherisc.

How do people make money in DeFi?

There's quite a method that folks are trying to maximize the expansion of DeFi. One strategy is generating passive income using Ethereum-based lending apps. Essentially users loan out their money and generate interest from the loans. Another strategy getting used is yield farming, a riskier practice by more advanced traders, during which users scan through a multitude of DeFi tokens in the hopes of finding opportunities for larger returns. Still, It is complicated and may lack transparency.

How risky is DeFi?

Like all other new decentralized blockchain networks trading in cryptocurrencies, DeFi is extremely risky, especially as you employ a new technology that aims to disrupt a longtime institution like a centralized bank. It is even riskier for beginners lured by the potential gains of yield farming and passive income. Ethereum has security and scam prevention guidelines as there also are broader potential risks.

Fraud and crime continue to be a big issue; consistent with calculations by blockchain data platform Chainalysis, $14 billion in cryptocurrency was sent to illicit addresses in 2021, nearly double the figure seen in 2020.

About $2.2 billion was outright stolen from DeFi protocols in 2021. While the analysis suggests cybercriminals raked in $7.8 billion in cryptocurrency from victims, about $2.8 billion of that figure came from a scam they call 'rug pulls.' In these scams, developers create apparently legitimate cryptocurrency projects before stealing investor money and disappearing.

Chainalysis warned that many of the attacks on DeFi exchanges over the past year are often traced back to errors within the smart contract code governing those protocols, which hackers exploit to steal funds.

Chapter 8 - Smart Contracts

Contracts regulate most facets of our professional and private lives and are essential to the functioning of society. As an overview of Blockchain technology, Smart Contracts play a really essential role; it helps to form the transactions happening more safe and secure and perform in an organized manner. And not just that, it helps other components like applications running on these platforms be even more accessible. But what's a smart contract? Decipher the worldwide craze surrounding Blockchain, Bitcoin, and cryptocurrencies with the Blockchain Certification.

What Is Smart Contract?

Smart contracts are computer programs or protocols for automated transactions stored on a blockchain and run in response to certain conditions. In other words, smart contracts automate the execution of agreements so that all participants can ascertain the result as soon as possible without an intermediary or time delay. Smart contracts are self-executing contracts during which the contents of the buyer-seller agreement are inscribed directly into lines of code. According to Nick Szabo, an American scientist who devised a virtual currency called "Bit Gold" in 1998, Smart contracts are computerized transaction protocols that execute contract conditions. Using it makes the transactions traceable, irreversible, and transparent. Caltech Blockchain Bootcamp Learn how to line up private Blockchain networks.

```solidity
// SPDX-License-Identifier: GPL-3.0


// Contributors
// Manager
// minContribution
//deadline
//target
//raiseAmount
//noOfContributors

pragma solidity >=0.4.0 <0.9.0;

contract CrowdFunding{
    mapping (address => uint) public Contributors;
    address public Manager;
    uint public minContribution;
    uint public deadline;
    uint public target;
    uint public raiseAmount;
    uint public noOfContributors;

    struct Request{
        string description;
        address payable recipient;
        uint value;
        bool isCompleted;
        uint noOfVoters;
        mapping (address=>bool) voters;

    }

    mapping (uint=>Request) public requests;
    uint public numRequests;

    constructor(uint _target , uint _deadline){
        target = _target;
        deadline = block.timestamp + _deadline;
        minContribution =100 wei;
        Manager = msg.sender;

    }


    function sendEth() public payable{
        require(block.timestamp < deadline ,"deadline has been passed");
        require(msg.value >= 100 wei , "Minimum Contribution is not met") ;

        if(Contributors[msg.sender] ==0){
            noOfContributors++;
        }
```

Figure 3- Example of a Smart Contract

Benefits of Smart Contracts

Accuracy, Speed, and Efficiency The contract is instantly executed when a condition is met. Because smart contracts are digital and automatic, there's no paperwork to affect, and No time was spent correcting errors that will occur when filling out documentation by hand.

Trust and Transparency

There's no got to worry about information being tampered with for private gain because there is no third party engaged, and Encrypted transaction logs are exchanged among participants.

Security

Because blockchain transaction records are encrypted, they are extremely difficult to hack. Furthermore, because each entry on a distributed ledger is linked to the entries before and after it, hackers would need to change the whole chain to vary one record. Savings Smart contracts eliminate the necessity for intermediaries to conduct transactions because of the time delays and costs accompanying them.

How Do Smart Contracts Work?

A smart contract may be a kind of program that encodes business logic and operates on a fanatical virtual machine embedded in a blockchain or other distributed ledger.

Step 1: Business teams collaborate with developers to define their criteria for the smart contract's desired behavior in response to specific events or circumstances.

Step 2: Conditions like payment authorization, shipment receipt, or a utility meter reading threshold are samples of simple events.

Step 3: More complex operations, like determining the worth of a derivative financial instrument, or automatically releasing an insurance payment, could be programmed using more complex logic.

Step 4: The developers then utilize a smart contract writing platform to make and test the logic. After the appliance is written, it is sent to a separate team for security testing.

Step 5: an indoor expert or a corporation that focuses on vetting smart contract security might be used.

Step 6: Once authorized, the contract is deployed on an existing blockchain or distributed ledger infrastructure.

Step 7: The smart contract is designed to concentrate on event updates from an "oracle," which is effectively a cryptographically secure streaming data source once deployed.

Step 8: Once it obtains the required combination of events from one or more oracles, the smart contract executes.

Smart Contacts and Flight Insurance

Let's consider a real-life scenario during which smart contracts are used. Rachel is at the airport, and her flight is delayed. AXA, an insurance firm, provides flight delay insurance utilizing Ethereum smart contracts. This insurance compensates Rachel in such a case. How? The smart contract is linked to the database recording flight status. The smart contract is made supported by terms and conditions. The condition set for the policy may be a delay of two hours or more. Supporting the code, the smart contract holds AXA's money until that certain condition is met. The smart contract is submitted to the nodes on EMV (a runtime compiler to execute the smart contract code)

for evaluation. All the nodes on the network executing the code must come to an equivalent result. That result's recorded on the distributed ledger. If the flight is delayed by more than two hours, the smart contract self-executes, and Rachel is compensated. Smart contracts are immutable; nobody may alter the agreement.

Voting and Blockchain

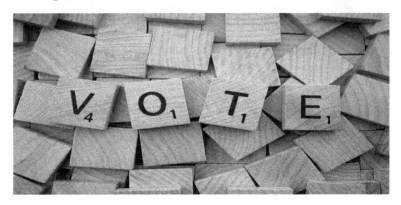

Implementation of Smart Contracts Using Blockchain within the voting process can eliminate common problems. A centralized electoral system faces difficulties when it involves tracking votes – identity fraud, miscounts, or bias by voting officials. In employing a smart contract, certain predefined terms and conditions are pre-set within the contract. No voter can vote from a digital identity aside from his or her own. The counting is foolproof. Every vote is registered on a blockchain network; therefore, the counting is tallied automatically with no intervention from a 3rd party or dependency on a manual process. Each ID is attributed to only one vote. Validation is accomplished by the users on the blockchain network itself. Thus, the voting process is often during a public blockchain, or it might be during a decentralized autonomous organization-based blockchain setup. As a result, every vote is recorded on the ledger, and therefore the information can not be modified. That ledger is publicly available for audit and verification.

Smart contracts allow you to make voting systems during which you will change voting rules, add and take away members, change debating periods, or alter the bulk rule. For example, you will create a vote for a choice within a decentralized autonomous organization. Instead of a central authority making a choice, a voting mechanism within the organization can decide whether the proposal is rejected or accepted.

Blockchain Implementation of a smart contract and Crowdfunding

Ethereum-based smart contracts could also be used to create digital tokens for performing transactions. You will design and issue your own digital currency, creating a tradable computerized token. The tokens use a typical coin API. Within the case of Ethereum, there are standardizations of ERC 2.0, allowing the contract to access any wallet for exchange automatically. As a result, you build a tradable token with a hard and fast supply. The platform becomes a financial institution of sorts, issuing digital money. Suppose you would like to start out a business requiring funding. But who would lend money to someone they do not know or trust? Smart contracts have a serious role to play. With Ethereum, you will build a smart contract to carry a contributor's funds until a given date passes or a goal is met. Supported the result, the funds are released to the contract owners or sent back to the contributors.

The centralized crowdfunding system has many issues with management systems. To combat this, a DAO (Decentralized Autonomous Organization) is employed for crowdfunding. The terms and conditions are set within the contract, and each individual participating in crowdfunding is given a token. Every contribution is recorded on the Blockchain. Limitation of Smart Contracts Because smart contracts can not send HTTP queries, they can not acquire information about "real-world" events. Using external data could endanger consensus, which is vital for security and decentralization.

Use Cases of Smart Contracts

The use cases for smart contracts range from minimal to complex. They can be used for easy economic transactions, like moving money from point A to point B, and for smart access management within the sharing economy. Smart contracts could disrupt many industries. Banking, insurance, energy, e-government, telecommunications, music, art, mobility, education, and many other industries have use cases.

Amending and Terminating Smart Contracts

Currently, there's no simple path to amend a sensible contract, creating certain challenges for contracting parties. For instance, during a traditional text-based contract, if the parties have mutually agreed to vary the parameters of their deal, or if there's a change in law, the parties can quickly draft an amendment to deal with that change or just modify their course of conduct.

Smart contracts currently do not offer such flexibility. In fact, as long as blockchains are immutable, modifying a smart contract is way more complicated than modifying standard software code that does not reside on a blockchain. The result's that amending a smart contract may yield higher transaction costs than amending a text-based contract and increases the margin of error that the parties would not accurately reflect the modifications they need to form. Similar challenges exist with reference to terminating a sensible contract. Assume a celebration discovers a mistake in an agreement that provides the counterparty more rights than intended or concludes that fulfilling its stated obligations will be much more costly than expected. During a text-based contract, a celebration can engage in, or threaten, so-called "efficient breach," i. e., knowingly breaching a contract and paying the resulting damages if it determines that the value to perform is bigger than the damages it might owe.

Moreover, a celebration may bring the counterparty back to the table to barter an agreeable resolution by ceasing performance or threatening to require that step. Smart contracts do not yet offer analogous self-help remedies. Projects are currently underway to make smart contracts that are terminable at any time and more easily amended. While this is often antithetical to the immutable and automatic nature of smart contracts, it reflects the fact that smart contracts will only gain commercial acceptance if they reflect the business reality of how contracting parties act.

The Limits of Incorporating Vagueness Into Smart Contracts

The objectivity and automation required of smart contracts can run opposite to how business parties actually negotiate agreements. During negotiations, parties implicitly engage during an analysis, knowing that at some point, there are diminishing returns in trying to consider and address every conceivable eventuality. These parties might not want to expend management time or legal fees on the negotiations or conclude that commencing revenue-generating activity under an executed contract outweighs addressing unresolved issues. Instead, they'll determine that if an unanticipated event occurs, they will find a resolution at that point. Similarly, parties may purposefully prefer to leave a somewhat ambiguous provision in an agreement to offer themselves the pliability to argue that the supply should be interpreted in their favor. This approach to contracting is rendered harder with smart contracts where code demands an exactitude not found within the negotiation of text-based contracts. A smart contract cannot include vague terms, nor can certain potential scenarios be left unaddressed.

Consequently, parties to smart contracts may find that the transaction costs of negotiating complex smart contracts surpass that of a standard text-based contract. It will take a while for those adopting smart contracts during a particular industry to work out which provisions are adequately objective to lend themselves to smart contract execution. As noted, to date, most smart contracts perform relatively simple tasks where the parameters of the "if/then" statements are clear. As smart contracts increase in complexity, parties may disagree on whether a specific contractual provision is often captured through the objectivity that a smart contract demands.

Do Smart Contracts Guarantee Payment?

One benefit often hyped about smart contracts is that they will automate payment without the necessity for collection expenses or dunning notices other and without the necessity to travel to court to get a judgment mandating payment. While this is often true for less complicated use cases, it will be less accurate in complex commercial relationships. The truth is that parties are constantly transferring funds around their organization and do not "park" total amounts that are due on a long-term accept anticipation of future payment requirements. Similarly, an individual obtaining a loan is unlikely to stay the complete loan amount during a specified wallet tied to the smart contract. Instead, the borrower will put those funds to use, funding the required repayments on a billboard on an ad-hoc basis. Suppose the owing party amounts under the smart contract fails to fund the wallet on a timely basis. In that case, a smart contract trying to transfer money from that wallet upon a trigger event may find that the required funds are unavailable. Implementing another layer into the method, like having the smart contract request to pull monies from other wallets, would not resolve the matter if those wallets or sources of funds also do not have the requisite payment amounts. The parties might seek to deal with this issue through a text-based requirement that a wallet linked to the smart contract always has a minimum amount, but that solution merely would give the party a greater legal argument if the dispute were adjudicated. It might not render the payment operation of the smart contract wholly automatic. Thus, although smart contracts will render payments much more efficient, they'll not eliminate the necessity to adjudicate payment disputes.

Risk Allocation for Attacks and Failures

Smart contracts introduce a further risk that does not occur in most text-based contractual relationships—the likelihood that the contract can be hacked or that the code or protocol may contain an unintended software error. These concepts are closely aligned with the comparative security of blockchains; most "hacks" related to blockchain technology are exploitations of an unintended coding error. Like many bugs in code, these errors aren't glaring but rather become obvious on just one occasion they need to be exploited.

For instance, in 2017, an attacker was ready to withdraw several multi-signature wallets offered by Parity of $31 million in ether. Multi-signature wallets combine a layer of security because they require one private key to access the wallet. However, within the Parity attack, the attacker was ready to exploit a flaw within the Parity code by reinitializing the smart contract and resulting in the attacker being the only owner of the multi-signature wallets.

Parties to a smart contract need to consider how liability and risk for inadvertent coding errors and resulting exploitations are distributed between the parties and possibly with any third-party developers or insurers of the smart contract.

Governing Law and Venue

One of the crucial promises of blockchain technology, and by extension, smart contracts, is the creation of strong, decentralized, and global platforms. However, global adoption means parties could also be employing a smart contract across much more jurisdictions than might exist within the case of text-based contracts. The party proposing terms under a smart contract would therefore be best served by indicating the venue and governing law for that smart contract.

A governing law stipulation specifies what basic law will apply to the interpretation of the smart contract, whereas a venue clause states which jurisdiction's courts will decide the dispute. In cases where the venue or governing law is not stipulated, a plaintiff could also be relatively unrestricted in choosing where to file a claim or in arguing which substantive law should apply, given the wide selection of jurisdictions during which a smart contract could be used.

As long as many early disputes concerning smart contracts are going to be ones of first impression, contracting parties will want some confidence surrounding where such disagreements will be adjudicated.

Best Practices

Given that we are at the emerging stages of smart contract adoption, best practices for implementing such code remain evolving. Nevertheless, the list below should help developers design effective smart contracts and guide companies who decide to use them. For now, parties entering into any sort of contractual arrangement would be best served by employing a hybrid approach that mixes text and code.

As stated, there are solid arguments that code-only smart contracts should be enforceable, a minimum of under-state jurisprudence within the U.S. However, until there's greater clarity on their validity and enforceability, code-only smart contracts should be used just for simpler transactions. Parties will still want text-versions of agreements to read the agreed-upon terms, memorialize terms that smart contracts aren't equipped to deal with, and have a record they know a court will uphold.

In a hybrid contract using code and plain text, the text should clearly identify the smart contract code with which It is associated. Consequently, the parties should have full visibility into the variables being transferred to the smart contract, how they are described, and the transaction actions that will trigger the execution of the code. When counting on oracles for off-chain data, the parties should address what would happen if the oracle is unable to obtrude the required data, provides erroneous data, or goes out of business. The parties should consider risk provision in the case of a coding error. The text contract accompanying the code should specify the governing law and venue because of the order of priority between text and code in the event of a conflict. The contract should include a representation by each party that they need to review the smart contract code, which reflects the terms found within the text contract. Although such a representation cannot compel a party to look at the code, it will help the counterparty protect against a claim that the code was never reviewed. Parties can also prefer to insure against the danger that the code contains errors. As noted, parties may need third-party experts to examine the code.

Future of Smart Contracts

Today, smart contracts are a classic example of "Amara's Law," the concept expressed by Stanford University scientist Roy Amara that we have an inclination to overestimate new technology within the short run and underestimate it at the end of the day. Although smart contracts will need to evolve before they are widely adopted for production use in complex commercial relationships, they need the impact to revolutionize the reward and incentive structure that shapes how parties accept the longer term. To that end, and when considering smart contracts, It is crucial to not simply think about how existing concepts and structures are often ported over to the present new technology. Rather, the true transformation of smart contracts will come from entirely new concepts we've not yet envisioned.

Chapter 9 - Blockchain Platforms

What is a blockchain platform?

Blockchain platforms or blockchain frameworks serve as the building blocks for developing blockchain-based applications. The following are several of the best know Blockchain platforms (Lawton, 2022).

Ethereum Blockchain

Ethereum may be a decentralized blockchain-based software that has smart contract capabilities. Ethereum is open source and used primarily to support the second-largest cryptocurrency within the world, referred to as Ether. Ethereum facilitates the smart contracts and applications built on its blockchain to run efficiently without control, downtime, fraud, or any third-party interaction.

Ethereum is also a programming language that assists developers in making distributed applications. One of the main projects with Ethereum is Microsoft's partnership with ConsenSys offering Ethereum Blockchain as a Service on Microsoft Azure to facilitate developers and enterprise clients to possess a cloud-based one-click blockchain developer environment.

Ethereum was forked into two blockchains in 2016: Ethereum and Ethereum Classic. This was thanks to a hack earlier that year during which the hacker stole $50 million Ether. The hacker leveraged of a third-party project shortcoming and exploited a DOA (a smart contract set originating from the Ethereum platform).

Ethereum was already the second-largest digital currency within the market as of September 2019. Ethereum's idea is to refurbish the use of applications on the web today. Today, many third-party intermediaries help us perform the tasks we would like to on the web.

As a result, essential data like users' financial data of varied applications are stored on servers controlled by these third parties. This suggests that the third parties are on top of things of the information and may do anything with and to the information without the user's consent. Furthermore, it poses a substantial risk concerning hacker attacks.

How to make use of Ethereum

Blockchain is decentralized because it is a public ledger that is not stored in a single location. The general public ledger is stored on thousands of volunteers' computers around the globe, each of which is named a node. Verifying the information stored on blockchain involves almost half the nodes before being certified as correct. Cryptography is employed to keep transactions on the blockchain network secure and verify them (Bellaj Badr, 2018).

Computers are wont to solve complex mathematical equations that help to verify transactions on the network and input new blocks into the chain.

Like other cryptocurrencies, Ether is often used as a digital currency in financial transactions. Ether also is a medium through which users can perform any task on Ethereum.

Ethereum aims to supply a system that gives users more control over their data and allows applications to be built and run on the blockchain. To run these applications and have this level of control on the Ethereum platform, it requires Ether. The more the amount of individuals making use of the platform, the higher the fees.

How to store Ether

To store Ether, a user needs an Ethereum wallet. Most of those wallets are digital and may be accessed via a laptop or smartphone. The Ethereum wallet stores the private key (secret keys with which the user can access the Ether) of the user.

If a user loses their private key, they will also lose their Ether, and there's nothing like a help desk or customer care to contact to recover your private key.

There are various sorts of wallets.

Hardware wallets are electronic devices like USB sticks that will be used to sign and send ether transactions without being online. They are detached from the web and provide a better security level. It is tough to hack, and It is best suited to store an outsized amount of Ether. On the downside, hardware wallets can stray a bit like the other key.

Desktop and Mobile wallets: Desktop wallets are wallets that run on a laptop or a PC, while Mobile wallets run on a smartphone. These wallets are often either custodial or non-custodial. Custodial wallets depend upon third parties to keep a user's private key safe. On the other hand, this has risks as these third parties are often hacked. Non-custodial wallets do not depend upon third parties to safeguard their private keys, they are kept safe by the user.

Paper wallets: This option involves printing or writing down the private key on an error of paper and keeping it safe somewhere. It is the foremost old-fashioned method of storage. The sole thing about this is often that you simply must remember where It is kept.

Web wallets are the smallest amount of safe storage methods involving storing private keys online.

A wallet connected to the web is named hot storage, while a wallet that is not connected to the web is named cold storage. Mixing the cold and hot storage wallets is advisable to urge maximum security.

How to buy Ether

Online Exchange platforms: This is typically the simplest method of shopping for cryptocurrencies. It entails a platform that buys and sells Ether for a fee. You will buy Ether from these platforms with fiat currency (dollar, Euro, pounds) with a bank transfer, debit, or MasterCard. The platforms follow the Know-Your-Customer (KYC) laws, which suggest that a user's identity must be confirmed before the user can transact on the platform. An example of such a platform is Coinbase.

Trading platforms: These platforms connect sellers and buyers via an intermediary, and they also can trade a cryptocurrency for an additional one.

Peer-to-peer: This method involves the customer contacting the vendor directly and negotiating prices. There's no middle man involved during this process, and there are not any fees paid. Some cities like Toronto and New York have Ethereum meetups frequently. Some sites like LocalCryptos help connect users who want to trade Ether through peer-to-peer methods.

How Ethereum Works

smart-contracts-vs-traditional-contracts
Any third party or entity does not control Ethereum. Instead, they are controlled by codes. Several pieces are close to making sure that Ethereum is operating accordingly.

Smart Contracts: The whole point of Ethereum having a system not controlled by a third party but by codes is generated by smart contracts. Smart contracts are automatically performed when certain stated conditions are met without the assistance of any external body. Smart contracts are involved in any cryptocurrency. They are not restricted to and may be used outside Ethereum, but they are popularly known for his or her Ethereum usage. Bitcoin also supports basic smart contracts, but its applications are narrow in comparison to Ethereum's. Some developers and researchers have criticized smart contracts, stating that they would open up possibilities for security vulnerabilities.

Ethereum Blockchain: This is where the history of all the smart contracts executed is stored. Many nodes from everywhere on the planet store a replica of the whole blockchain. Thousands of computers handle a smart contract whenever it is executed to ensure that each stated rule is followed. The nodes not only store transaction details but also store accounts, smart contract code, smart contract state. All the nodes follow an equivalent rule set for verifying a transaction and that they are all connected.

Ethereum Virtual Machine (EVM): The Ethereum virtual machine performs smart contracts. It helps translate the smart contract written by a language computer that can not read to a language (bytecode) that they will read. The EVM can execute a minimum of 140 different codes with specific tasks.

Ether: As already stated, Ether is Ethereum's native cryptocurrency. Ether is stored in accounts, and there are two sorts of accounts. Externally owned accounts are utilized to hold and transfer Ether by users, and Contract accounts are the accounts that hold smart contracts.

Proof-of-Work: When a block of a transaction is made, miners, in an effort to urge the right value of the block, generate values until they catch on. A hash value is then transferred across the network for the nodes to validate when the miner discovers it. The miner receives the Ether once it finds the hash if it is validated. However, there is an idea to modify to a replacement algorithm called proof-of-stake, designed to consume less electricity and computing power than proof-of-work.

Figure 4- Example of Ethereum Blockchain

Ethereum Use Cases

Decentralized Finance (Defi): Decentralized finance may be used for financial services and products that are accessible and available to anyone who will use Ethereum. No authority can refuse access to anything, block payments or users, and markets are always open. Anyone can examine the codes, and there are not any longer risks of human errors because the services are now governed by code and are automatic. With traditional finance, some problems that occur include:

- Denial of a person from making use of monetary services
- Financial services can prevent a person from getting paid.
- Restriction of trading hours to specific time zones trading hours
- Centralized institutions and governments can pack up the markets at will.

In the Defi system, the user holds and has total control over their own money; the transfer of funds takes just a couple of minutes, it is hospitable to anyone, and therefore the market is usually open. A user can also send money anywhere within the world, access stable currencies, trade tokes, buy insurance, borrow funds with or without collateral, and much more.

Non-Fungible Tokens (NFTs): NFTs are tokens that will be attached to unique items and aren't interchangeable with the other item. They permit value to tend to art, music, etc., in terms of digital currency. They are secured on the Ethereum blockchain and may have just one owner at a time. A replacement NFT can not be copied and pasted into existence; no two are often equivalent. They are compatible with anything that is built on the Ethereum platform. NFTs are often sold anywhere; therefore, the owners have access to the worldwide market.

Decentralized autonomous organizations (DAOs): DAOs are owned and governed collectively by their members and function-supported smart contracts.

They are internet-based and have in-built treasuries that can not be accessed without permission by the group. They create decisions by proposals and voting to ensure everybody within the group can air their opinions. There's no CEO or CFO, so the rules governing their spending are part of the DAO code. The codes and everyone their actions are transparent and operate a democratic system. The votes which are tallied automatically are required before any changes are often implemented. Samples of DAOs are charity organizations, ventures, freelancer networks, etc.

How OriginStamp uses the Ethereum blockchain

Ethereum is an append-only ledger like other blockchains, and any data stored inside It is secured against manipulation. OriginStamp uses the Ethereum blockchain together with the blockchains to make tamper-proof, blockchain-based timestamps. OriginStamp timestamps can then prove that a document or digital asset existed at a selected time and hasn't changed since. The newest Event API from

OriginStamp also uses Ethereum to make transparent, not alterable, Event chains.

Hyperledger Blockchain

What is Hyperledger Fabric?

Hyperledger Fabric may be a private blockchain framework and is one among many projects within the Hyperledger blockchain platform (Bellaj Badr, 2018). The framework is employed as a foundation from which to develop blockchain-based applications, networks, and more. Fabric (as often shortened) was designed to create private blockchains that will be used within one organization or group of aligned organizations that link to other blockchain implementations. Fabric prioritizes several key features as a part of its architecture:

Privacy: Fabric requires all computers within its network to be identified; the potential members of a cloth-supported network must join and identify themselves via a Membership Service Provider (MSP).

This is often what's called a "permissioned" membership. Maintaining the privacy of knowledge is important to several industries, and this aspect alone makes Fabric a beautiful option. It is important to notice that Fabric does not require all parts of a blockchain to be permissioned; the need for permissions is set at the discretion of whoever designs the network.

Channels: Fabric allows partitioning ledgers into "channels," where network members may create separate transactions that aren't visible to the larger network. This enables more sensitive data to be segregated from nodes that do not require access.

Scalability: Another appealing characteristic of cloth for larger enterprises is the immensely scalable network that Fabric provides. Like other implementations, the amount of nodes participating within the network can quickly scale; but the system is capable of still processing large amounts of knowledge with a smaller set of resources. This enables for a better of both worlds approach. The blockchain is often created with a little set of nodes and scales on demand.

Modularity: Fabric's architecture permits separate components to be added and implemented at different times. Many components are optional and may be omitted completely or introduced later without affecting functionality. This feature is meant to offer a corporation power over what's and is not necessary to implement. A number of the components considered modular, or "plug-and-play," includes the tactic of attaining consensus, the ledger store itself, specific access APIs, membership services for identification, and chaincode integration.

To develop an incredibly scalable, permissioned, and secure framework powered by blockchain's distributed ledger technology, Hyperledger Fabric is poised to require the planet of corporate networks by storm. Fabric is already finding itself in the middle of some incredible industry projects.

What Hyperledger Fabric is not

With some idea of what Fabric provides, it is also important to know what Fabric is not. Hyperledger Fabric may be a blockchain framework. It works alongside other Hyperledger projects like Burrow and Sawtooth to supply a scalable data platform. Hyperledger Fabric could also be a platform on which applications may be developed. Like Composer, Quilt, and Explorer, other ecosystem members utilize data from Fabric networks.

Hyperledger Platforms

Hyperledger Burrow: A modular client designed to operate as a permission Ethereum smart contract interpreter as a node on a blockchain. Burrow executes smart contract code on an Ethereum Virtual Machine. Burrow is not considered a fix-all or highly pluggable.

Hyperledger Sawtooth: This modular Hyperledger platform is meant for generating and deploying blockchains; It is also a platform for coding applications to work together with the blockchain. It also supports a variety of various pluggable approaches to reaching consensus.

Together (or apart), Burrow, Sawtooth, and Fabric platforms are either clients or were created to advance the designing, implementation, and deployment of applications, clients, and blockchain solutions.

Hyperledger Tools

Hyperledger Composer: Composer was a set of tools for constructing the particular blockchain network employed by Hyperledger platforms (primarily Fabric). Since August 2019, Composer has been phased out of use, and therefore the functionality provided by Composer has been folded into Fabric itself.

Hyperledger Quilt: Quilt may be a Hyperledger tool meant to facilitate the transfer of transactions between different blockchain networks and even between blockchains and non-distributed networks. This is often made possible by using the Interledger protocol.

Hyperledger Explorer: This tool was developed primarily for accessing equally data within a blockchain network; the querying of blocks, accessing transactional data, members and respective nodes, information about the network itself, and almost everything that is a part of that specific blockchain.

In this sense, it becomes easier to ascertain the entire role of cloth within a blockchain network's functionality. Whereas Fabric may be a platform that permits for the definition, acceptance, and construction of knowledge, the tools under the Hyperledger project are pitched toward accessing and consuming the information of a blockchain.

A Note on Hyperledger and Cryptocurrency

A central facet of Hyperledger is that Hyperledger is not a cryptocurrency as a project. It did not use cryptocurrency in any form and was purposefully designed in this manner. Hyperledger is developed simply to advance blockchain technology and provide a strong implementation of highly scalable data storage technology. Fabric, of course, is simply a blockchain framework under the umbrella project.

It is important to remember that blockchain provides just the inspiration for an immutable database with a distributed ledger and successively for a decentralized sort of currency to be developed. Blockchain itself is not Bitcoin or cryptocurrency generally. Hyperledger Fabric takes the inspiration of blockchain and provides a framework on top of it, utilizing its qualities as a network. In this context, Cryptocurrency may be a specific application of the technology instead of the first motivation.

Understanding that Hyperledger does not believe in a "proof of work" system that involves bitcoin mining, and by circumventing a reliance on any sort of crypto (unlike blockchain frameworks under Ethereum), Fabric is more interesting to enterprises looking to adopt a replacement sort of business-to-business transaction networking instead of an entirely new currency.

Fabric Smart Contracts (Chaincode)

Smart contracts (frequently mentioned within Hyperledger Fabric as chaincode), alongside the ledger, are the foremost vital aspects of a cloth network. In the blockchain, smart contracts combat the role of lawyers, helping to trade funds, goods, or whatever other assets are characterized within the network. These contracts establish prices, layout rules, outline agreements, and even delegate actions to be done when certain requirements are met. These are often limitless and simple: paying a particular amount, getting a refund if goods aren't delivered, or giving digital receipts. These contracts happen within a blockchain as executable code.

These smart contracts combat a more familiar role within Fabric, acting because of the literal contracts prescribed between two professional entities when making a trade. Having smart contracts significantly simplifies the method of trading by automating processes and handling exchanges of payment. While the smart contract code manages executing all of the above, the chaincode is what deploys the smart contract into the network, so even though they are developed together, they tend to try various things.

```go
package main

import (
    "encoding/json"
    "fmt"
    "strconv"

    "github.com/hyperledger/fabric-chaincode-go/shim"
    sc "github.com/hyperledger/fabric-protos-go/peer"
    "github.com/hyperledger/fabric/common/flogging"
)

// SmartContract Define the Smart Contract structure
type SmartContract struct {
}

// Car :  Define the car structure, with 4 properties.  Structure tags are used by encoding/json libra
type Car struct {
    Make   string `json:"make"`
    Model  string `json:"model"`
    Colour string `json:"colour"`
    Owner  string `json:"owner"`
}

// Init ;  Method for initializing smart contract
func (s *SmartContract) Init(APIstub shim.ChaincodeStubInterface) sc.Response {
    return shim.Success(nil)
}

var logger = flogging.MustGetLogger("fabcar_cc")

// Invoke :  Method for INVOKING smart contract
func (s *SmartContract) Invoke(APIstub shim.ChaincodeStubInterface) sc.Response {

    function, args := APIstub.GetFunctionAndParameters()

    logger.Infof("Function name is:  %d", function)
    logger.Infof("Args length is : %d", len(args))

    if function == "queryCar" {
        return s.queryCar(APIstub, args)
    } else if function == "initLedger" {
        return s.initLedger(APIstub)
    } else if function == "createCar" {
        return s.createCar(APIstub, args)
    }
    return shim.Error("Invalid Smart Contract function name.")
}

func (s *SmartContract) queryCar(APIstub shim.ChaincodeStubInterface, args []string) sc.Response {

    if len(args) != 1 {
        return shim.Error("Incorrect number of arguments. Expecting 1")
```

Figure 5- Example of Hyperledger

Hyperledger Fabric Components

Similar to all blockchain-based technologies or platforms, Hyperledger Fabric is made upon a couple of main modules:

- a distributed ledger for all data recorded about the transactions
- multiple peers (or nodes)
- smart contracts that maintain transaction logic

Also, similar to most blockchain networks, transactions must be approved by a consensus of all nodes to be entered into the ledger. In Fabric, this is often mentioned as an endorsement.

Figure 6- Hyperledger Components

Peers (or Nodes)

Peers themselves represent organizations and members. Peers play an essential role within a blockchain network -- that is, they host instances of ledgers and smart contracts. This way, peers are most significant during a Fabric blockchain concerning transactions or the transaction workflow.

When a transaction is to require a place, the transaction must first be confirmed by a majority of the members of a network (represented as endorser peers) or a channel within a network. This process has been named the consensus.

In addition to consensus, peers combat additional roles within the transaction workflow. Within a channel, they act as modules and supply infrastructure for the movement and processing of knowledge. Some samples of these roles consist of:

Orderer Peers - The peers (or nodes) that are particularly designated as orderers ensure that all the peers within a channel have an equivalent revised ledger. In this case, orderer peers ensure consistency of knowledge and protect the integrity of the ledger. Orderers also construct the blocks after the endorsement of a transaction and enter the record into them. When working in cohesion, the orderer peers, collectively called the ordering service, send the new blocks to every peer within a channel to update their respective ledgers. The ordering service is a modular element. It is important to understand that there are several methods for implementing this ordering service within a cloth network:

Solo - The Solo method is made upon utilizing just one orderer node within a network. It is simple to line up and even as easy to manage. This is often useful for development environments, although it becomes a choke point in larger networks. Worse, the solo method offers zero security in crash tolerance, which puts production data in danger. As such, Solo is merely recommended for development and testing purposes. It is advised not to design upon Solo during a project during which you plan to expand later.

Raft - Raft implementations are compatible with getting used as one node for both development and expanded to multiple nodes within a production environment. Raft also incorporates some built-in crash fault tolerance. Raft implementations are also simpler than fixing Kafka nodes and infrequently versatile in deployment.

Kafka - Used primarily for production, Kafka may be a sturdy distributed streaming platform which will publish to records, process records, and store records. Similar to Raft deployments, Kafka is crash-tolerant. This comes at the cost of requiring that the Kafka cluster be deployed and managed.

Endorser Peers - Peers are often designated within the Endorser role. This is often in the transaction workflow to either refuse it outright or approve a transaction request as valid and accept it to the ledger. They handle the execution of chaincode to try to do so.

Each peer has its own updated copy of the distributed ledger and the facility of executing the chaincode for endorsement.

Hyperledger Fabric CA

The Hyperledger Fabric CA (or Fabric Certificate Authority) acts because of the Membership Service Provider for Hyperledger Fabric. It handles the registration of members, regulation of nodes, and certification. In essence, certificate authorities perform a significant role in making Fabric a permissioned blockchain, removing deprecated accounts, and registering members, keeping track of identities within the network.

The Hyperledger Fabric CA server communicates with elements of the material network via REST APIs, which successively interact with either a cloth SDK that the client application was designed with or a special instance of the material CA client. The material CA is an optional, modular component. More information could also be found within the official documentation.

Fabric CA Diagram

As a modular component of cloth, the Certificate Authority resides on a separate node than that of the remainder of the network and helps to mediate secure interactions.

Ledger

The distributed ledger is the critical element that makes blockchain special. This ledger is at the middle of what Hyperledger Fabric is all about. Within this ledger, you will find every record of each transaction ever performed within a channel of the network, including details of a few given transactions. These details include when the transaction occurred, whom, what proportion it had been for, what it had been for, and almost anything you could possibly want to understand. This ledger (or ledgers, rather) also protects the safety of this data through blockchains' famous immutability. Once added into the ledger, data can not be modified in any way.

Ledgers are composed of blocks of knowledge. Their most vital components include an ID, an up-to-date hash of the integrated transactions, and therefore the hash of the previous block upon which the present relies.

Interestingly, the blocks within the ledger keep a record of all endorsed and successfully entered transactions, including people who were rejected during the endorsement process. This prevents re-submission and re-evaluation of already unapproved attempted transactions.

Hyperledger Fabric Workflow

How do cloth components work together to enable the write, read, and processing of data?

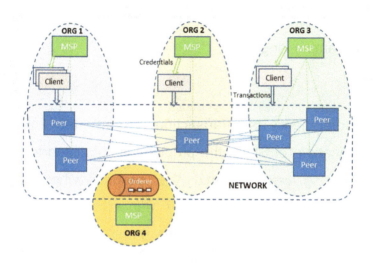

Figure 7- Hyperledger Basic Network

Transaction Processing

Fabric uses checks and verification to assist validate data before submission to the chain for every transaction; these steps include:

Creation of transaction proposal: Imagine a trade, like a deal between an automobile company and a car dealership. The lifetime of this transaction starts with its establishment by a network peer. The peer creates a proposal within a client application connected to the network written against the SDK of a specific programing language.

Endorsement of transaction: From the client application (or SDK), the proposal is submitted to the endorsing peers (within the channel where the transaction takes place) for endorsement. Each endorsing peer performs the proposal (a function defined within the chaincode) and returns a positive or negative response. The responses and results from the chaincode are returned to the client.

Submission to orderer peers: After being endorsed and returned, the transaction is then submitted to the ordering service (or combined group of ordering peers/nodes), which uses consensus to order the transaction into a block within the ledger. Note that, unlike other blockchain frameworks, the ordering (block storage) of a validated transaction into the ledger is final - this suggests that the transactions storage within the block is unchangeable and that the block's place within the ledger also ensures a replacement level of immutability.

Commitment of transaction: Once requested, the stored transaction block is shipped to all or any of the peers as a part of the channel. This is a final validation step before changes are literally made to the ledger. There could also be quite one transaction stored within one among these blocks.

Submission to ledger: Once the transaction(s) within the block sent back to the peers is ratified and finalized, the block is written into the ledger.

R3 Corda Blockchain

What is R3 and Corda?

With legacy banks and large corporations eyeing the crypto space with increasing interest, R3's Corda blockchain allows large enterprise systems to adopt blockchain technology simply. Many decentralized finance (DeFi) folks dreams of a "bankless" world filled with transparency and decentralization.

However, it is worth adding that disrupting enterprise systems may be a massively ambitious goal. After all, with the trillions of dollars these entities control, It is unlikely they are just getting to lay down and let DeFi devour them. That is why R3 founders Todd McDonald and David E. Rutter have put their hopes on a hybrid potential for the blockchain – a blockchain that is neither wholly transparent nor completely decentralized.

R3's founders combined hold over 50 years of experience in capital markets and financial services.

As such, they share a considerable amount of business know-how and experience. Their long careers taught them about the intense lack of trust between large firms and the way they transact amongst themselves and collaborate. Therefore, they figured if large enterprises would not go fully decentralized, they might have a minimum of subsided centralized and more connected through blockchain technology.

They believed that if they might find out how to deliver blockchain solutions to the present sector, it could transform whole industries. Therefore, R3 developed Corda – a distributed ledger technology platform that has created many blockchain networks for the insurance, banking, and trade finance industries.

The R3 Corda Vision

R3's team thinks that with multi-party applications, they will assist with creating a digitally connected world. They strive to create solutions that help build trust across the financial services ecosystem. The network effect can multiply blockchain benefits and encourage industries to return together.

Nevertheless, R3 has also challenged the notion that blockchains must transmit data to all parties. Furthermore, they are skeptical that companies will want to dispose of all their current technology for the blockchain. Nor will they risk coding their applications in untested blockchain languages.

That is why R3 decided to create Corda on the Java Virtual Machine (JVM). The JVM enables computers to run programs written within the Java programing language and languages it can compile to Java. The selection of JVM is certainly in stark contrast to what most platforms use when onboarding to the blockchain, like Solidity or Vyper.

Blockchain Benefits

It is no secret that this economic system sits atop an ancient infrastructure. Transactions are costly, complex, and susceptible to fraud and human error. It is still a paper-based system requiring local data storage and intermediaries for validation.

However, with the blockchain, peers share one ledger, and after a transaction gets validated, the record is secure and immutable. Additionally, smart contracts run on top of the blockchain containing rules to which mutual parties agree. This factor eliminates the necessity for 3rd parties. Among other things, the sweetness of blockchain technology is that it lets each transaction side know what occurred and when.

The Benefits of DeFi

After all, the software has been eating the planet for a few times, but it hasn't done an excellent job disrupting financial services. That is mainly due to entrenched incumbents, regulatory constraints, and high switching costs. As a result, while fintech has offered traditional finance a UX facelift, many of the underlying systems developed within the 1970s continue to be in place.

Furthermore, DeFi dApps will replace legal enforcement with smart contracts, cumbersome paperwork with code, and humans with machines. We all know that DeFi can run circles around its analog ancestors, especially regarding costs. That is because the worldwide blockchain and interoperability are replacing the antiquated, siloed transaction systems of traditional banking.

Blockchain and Distributed Ledger Technology

People often use the terms "Blockchain" and "Distributed Ledger Technology" (DLT) interchangeably. But to know blockchain technology, and more specifically R3's Corda blockchain, It is essential to know the underlying DLT framework.

A distributed ledger may be a database. However, unlike the centralized database employed by traditional enterprises, a distributed ledger exists across multiple sites and participants. Thus It is no single point of failure nor the necessity for a central authority or intermediaries common to the centralized database.

Companies use distributed ledger technology to validate transactions; therefore, the ledger's participants can examine all the records. It, therefore, provides an auditable history of a specific dataset.

So, once you attempt to distinguish between blockchain technology and DLT, consider the blockchain as a kind of DLT. The foremost significant difference is that a blockchain consists of a sequence of blocks, while DLT does not need such a sequence.

Thus you will say that every blockchain is DLT, but not all DLT are blockchains. Blockchains are but a kind and a subset of distributed ledgers.

Is Corda a Blockchain?

Corda may be a blockchain by definition; transactions get cryptographically chained to the transactions dependent upon them. However, there's one important differentiator: Corda does not batch transactions into a block before approving them. Rather, Corda approves each transaction immediately in real-time.

So, with Corda, there's no got to await a block interval. This factor increases scalability and privacy. Thus, Corda may be a hybrid, if you will. It is a blockchain; at the same time, it is not a blockchain.

R3 Corda Programs

With Corda, businesses can transact with smart contracts but with strict privacy. The Corda option decreases record-keeping and transaction costs while allowing companies to streamline their operations with such programs as:

1. CorDapps

R3 has many companies building applications on Corda, and these applications are called "CorDapps." CorDapps encourage developers to create permissioned distributed networks and to interact and connect with new partners.

2. Partner Connect Program

R3 features a Partner Connect Program to assist adopters to develop innovative solutions on Corda. Also, the program seeks to assist institutions in resolving real-world problems by adopting blockchain technology.

3. Launchpad

R3's Launchpad is for CorDapp builders that are in their early stages. Other Accelerator and Incubator programs for apps are within the later phases of development.

4. Venture Development

R3's Venture Development program aids users to get to market quickly and claims to possess over 350 institutions already building and deploying thereon.

5. Conclave

After Corda's triumph, R3 launched Conclave, a confidential platform to develop apps. It enables different parties to research and share data securely.

```java
package com.template.contracts;

import com.template.states.CarState;
import net.corda.core.contracts.Command;
import net.corda.core.contracts.CommandData;
import net.corda.core.contracts.Contract;
import net.corda.core.contracts.ContractState;
import net.corda.core.transactions.LedgerTransaction;
import org.jetbrains.annotations.NotNull;

import java.security.PublicKey;
import java.util.List;

// ************
// * Contract *
// ************
public class CarContract implements Contract {
    // This is used to identify our contract when building a transaction.
    public static final String CAR_CONTRACT_ID = "com.template.contracts.CarContract";

    @Override
    public void verify(@NotNull LedgerTransaction tx) throws IllegalArgumentException {

        if (tx.getCommands().size() != 1) throw new IllegalArgumentException("There can only be one command");

        Command command = tx.getCommand(0);
        CommandData commandType = command.getValue();
        List<PublicKey> requiredSigners = command.getSigners();

        if (commandType instanceof Shipment) {

            // Shipment Rules

            // Shape rules

            if (tx.getInputStates().size() != 0) {
                throw new IllegalArgumentException("There cannot be input states");
            }

            if (tx.getOutputStates().size() != 1 ) {
                throw new IllegalArgumentException("Only one vehicle can be shipped at a time");
            }

            // Content rules

            ContractState outputState = tx.getOutput(0);

            if (!(outputState instanceof CarState)) {
                throw new IllegalArgumentException("Output has to be of type CarState");
            }
```

Figure 8- Example of R3 Corda

R3 Corda Features

Below are a number of the highest features:

1. Data Privacy

Data transacted between parties on Corda is private. This feature may be a significant difference between permissionless blockchain networks.

2. Scalability

Corda is an adaptable platform designed to scale to a business's requirements. Users can start small on Corda and rapidly progress to Corda Enterprise.

3. Open Source

Corda is open source built on JVM.

4. Developer Community

Corda features a robust community of developers adding new functionality and features to the platform at a swift release tempo.

Permissioned vs. Permissionless Blockchains

Regardless of one's favorites, there are numerous use cases for both types. The most reason to use a permissioned system is to do with digital compliance. Whether it is financial, medical, or legal, the information sets in these use cases will demand a better level of privacy.

But the matter with many smart contract platforms is that they can not meet the privacy needs of those sorts of use cases. That is because the central premise behind blockchain is that It is permissionless, "be your own bank," and everyone that.

Libertarian Dreams vs. Regulated Reality

The libertarian dream of decentralization and transparency drove the first cypherpunks and crypto-anarchists who founded the space. Therefore, dreams of a bankless world persist. It is an idealistic world where people can trade freely without intermediaries and oversight, without useless go-betweens and central authorities asserting themselves between transactions to exact excessive fees.

On the opposite side of that coin, let's say that two parties want to transact privately with one another without their addresses broadcast on Ethereum. What if they might maintain a replica of the information on their respective servers but use the blockchain to urge consensus on the transaction? This example is where Corda steps in as a hybrid blockchain to urge public consensus while keeping the transaction private.

With Corda, the transaction data is merely available to the cooperating parties. Hence, users can interact with the network for performance while maintaining data privacy for his or her business or personal needs.

R3 Corda's Privacy Option

Yes, permissionless blockchains are incredible, but will legacy enterprises go alongside it? Or is it more probable they are going to enforce some sort of control, privacy, and centralization? Believe it? Would you would like your search history to be public? Or your medical history? Or all of your banking data? There's tons of knowledge floating around that folks will want to stay private.

Currently, Ethereum is pseudonymous, but with governments and personal firms like Chainalysis busily working to attach blockchain addresses to non-public individuals, it is even harder to take care of it.

Moreover, let's say a standard business wants to work on one of these blockchains.

1. Whom do they call if something goes amiss with the network?
2. What if there is a privacy concern?

These issues will stop participants from joining if they can not get the use cases out of their blockchain.

Understanding ISO

ISO, or the Independent Sales Organization, maybe a third-party payment processing company that handles businesses' merchant accounts. These ISOs aren't officially cardmember associates like VISA or MasterCard, but they partner with acquiring member banks to supply merchant services to members.

ISO 20022 is the new Swift standard for global payments as global trade becomes standardized. Anything outside the ISO standard will be suspect regarding the confines of the worldwide banking infrastructure.

R3 and CBDCs?

Various countries are determining whether or not to embrace a central bank-backed digital currency

(CBDC). CBDCs seek to be the digital equivalent of money for everyday end-users like businesses and households.

However, they differ from other cashless instruments since they represent an immediate claim on the financial institution instead of a personal institution. All in all, ISO 20022 migration will probably be positive for CBDCs and negative for a few cryptocurrencies.

But what does this need to do with R3 Corda? It is crucial because Corda is ISO compliant. Meaning It is well-positioned to serve these big players in finance.

Unfortunately for those curious about directly investing in R3 Corda, they didn't create a native token. That fact has opened the door for much speculation on which contender will achieve becoming the settlement token for Corda.

Corda, XDC, XLM, and XRP

And that leads us to XinFin's XDC, Stellar's XLM, and Ripple's XRP. These three projects come to mind when considering potential tokens for Corda. Although there are others, XDC, XLM, and XRP appear to be the foremost prominent. That is due to ISO compatibility.

The differences are that XDC is more about smart contracts while XRP and XLM are more about providing off-chain liquidity and micropayments. Thus, they need different functions but with some overlapping along the way.

Tribalism runs rampant in crypto, so we would not get into the talk over which of the three has the simplest chance of success. Additionally, since R3's Corda is already partnering with some of the most important names in central banking (along with the Nasdaq, MasterCard, Visa, and IBM, etc.), which becomes Corda's settlement token could reap significant rewards.

We've already covered XLM during a past article, and Ripple's lawsuit has left some people skeptical if XRP can recover. Meanwhile, XinFin is making inroads by becoming the primary to use of the DASL Crypto Bridge. DASL enables XDC to maneuver to Corda to contend for the prize of settlement tokens within the Corda ecosystem.

Corda's Future Ecosystem

With all the competition debate, there are those like XDC's new hot-shot developer, Quincy Jones, who consider the three projects more like collaborators than direct competition. He describes XDC, XLM, and XRP as "not even playing an equivalent sport. " whether or not they find yourself competing or complimenting each other in Corda's new financial ecosystem remains to be defined.

One thing is for certain; blockchain developers are still in high demand. XinFin's Quincy Jones has only been within the blockchain space for a brief while, and he's already becoming the "face of the franchise. " And you will do an equivalent if you are willing to figure not only hard but smart.

Quorum Blockchain

Quorum is one of the favored blockchain platforms that have recently gained promising popularity. Consequently, the interest in Quorum blockchain use cases has also been increasing profoundly in recent times.

Need for Quorum Blockchain

Smart contracts offer improved efficiency and reduced prices compared to the prevailing enterprise systems. The prevailing smart contract systems available with replicated shared ledgers do not have sufficient capabilities for offering data privacy. The smart contract state transactions and data are clearly visible on replicated shared ledger. Numerous setbacks like these have led to the evolution of the latest variations of smart contracts.

The new methodologies included homomorphic encryption, cryptographic protocols, zero-knowledge proofs, and many others. Quorum use cases are basically leveraging the facility of an easier approach towards privacy, with the essence of the Ethereum platform. Quorum retains numerous significant features of Ethereum, like increasing the general security of the network by revealing details of personal transactions to parties involved within the transaction. So, allow us to determine more about Quorum and what exactly It is before diving into the uses of Quorum blockchain.

Defining Quorum Blockchain

Quorum is essentially a personal or permissioned blockchain network supported by a fork of the Ethereum blockchain. The inspiration of Quorum is the Go implementation of Ethereum. It controls a voting-based consensus algorithm. The unique feature of Quorum, which ensures data privacy is that the new feature is referred to as a personal transaction identifier. The first design goal behind Quorum was reusing the utilization of existing technology to the maximum amount possible. Consequently, Quorum blockchain use cases would need to undergo limited changes to maintain sync with upcoming versions of the general public Ethereum codebase.

The majority of the logic underlying the Quorum blockchain focused on better privacy functionality is clear during a layer sitting aboard a typical Ethereum protocol layer. The elemental question 'Who is using Quorum?' should often come after reflecting on why enterprises and individuals should use Quorum. The core foundation of Quorum highlights using cryptography to stop unauthorized access to sensitive data and private transactions. The essential design of Quorum features the subsequent two elements.

A singular shared blockchain

Blend of alterations to Ethereum and smart contract software architecture. Smart contract architecture in Quorum provides functionalities of personal data separation. The modifications on the go-Ethereum codebase for Quorum also incorporate changes to the authentication processes and block proposals. The block validation process undergoes changes, such as that different nodes offer validation for public transactions.

However, in the case of personal transactions, only the nodes that are party to the transaction through execution of contract code associated with the transactions participate within the block validation process. Within the case of other transactions marked as private in certain Quorum use cases, the node can escape the method for contract code execution.

Architecture of Quorum Blockchain

The working of Quorum architecture depends on state database separation. The state database is replicated in two categories: public state database and private state database. The nodes within the network are maintained in perfect state consensus on the general public state. Within the case of personal state databases, differences would become plainly evident.

Yet if the client node state database could not store the state of the entire global state database, the distributed blockchain, alongside all transactions, enables the entire replication throughout all nodes and offers cryptographic security for immutability advantages. Thus, the uses of Quorum blockchain could find a singular advantage associated with other segmentation strategies on the idea of multiple blockchains. It also adds up to the safety and resilience of the design.

Who is Using Quorum?

The characteristics of Quorum and its basic design principle mean the possibilities of Quorum's varied productive use cases. However, after an in-depth overview of what Quorum Blockchain is, It is reasonable to wonder about "Who is using Quorum?" to learn more about its popularity. So, allow us to glance at several notable enterprises that use Quorum before moving toward its use cases.

- ING Group
- Ant Group
- Cargill
- Microsoft
- JP Morgan Chase
- LVMH
- HSBC
- Novartis

Additionally, Quorum is well prepared for continuous growth throughout different industries alongside Enterprise Ethereum. Consistent with the Forbes Top 50 list for 2021, Quorum can find promising applications with promising scope for growth in supply chain management, manufacturing, finance, and insurance.

Top 10 Quorum Blockchain Use Cases

The clarity regarding the essential functions of Quorum and its popularity within the enterprise landscape gives the right foundation to start discussing the uses of the Quorum blockchain. Let us take an in-depth check out the various samples of using Quorum across ten different sectors.

1. Banking and Finance

The most promising sector for locating Quorum blockchain utilization cases obviously points to financial services. Blockchain has been a prominent game changer within the field of monetary applications. Each Quorum example in several applications of Quorum within the financial services sector enhances the worth of blockchain in finance. Several of the foremost prominent use cases of Quorum blockchain in banking and finance include the subsequent applications.

- Tokenized cash
- Commercial bank payments
- Supply chain finance
- Exchanging information regarding sanctions
- Commodity post-trade processing
- Capital market data
- Interbank payments in association with central banks
- Trade finance
- Institutional trading
- Loan marketplaces and issuing debts

Besides these applications, the Quorum can also assist in developing a ledger system for auditing financial transactions. For instance, Block Ledger is an example of the utilization case of Quorum blockchain. It is essentially a decentralized accounting ledger system that leverages Quorum blockchain through the BaaS (Blockchain-as-a-Service) approach. The functions of Block Ledger specialize in rationalizing debtors and creditors through the addition of hash on the blockchain. This will be helpful for account reconciliation, transparency, risk and credit scoring, e-invoicing, and audit trail.

2. Insurance

The most common Quorum example within the insurance sector is State Farm. The first functionality of leveraging Quorum blockchain during this insurance use case emphasizes claim subrogation. State Farm leverages the services of Quorum blockchain together with the renowned insurer, USAA, for this use case. The blockchain insurance subrogation network could aid the increase of the rate of payments for auto-insurance claims.

The change of insurance claims to the blockchain network can substantially reduce the quantity of checks in conjunction with other paper-based processes between the two participating institutions. Replacing the prevailing insurance subrogation mechanisms could deliver promising improvements in efficiency. Blockchain might be helpful for introducing improvements like automation of carrier-to-carrier claims payments. As a result, it can provide significant savings in terms of cash and time. Using Quorum blockchain technology could ensure secure improvement and automation of manual processes. At an equivalent time, Quorum blockchain use cases within the insurance sector could also help ensure that cash travels faster to members and customers of an application.

3. Healthcare

Healthcare is another major sector for showcasing the uses of Quorum blockchain. The foremost notable example of using Quorum blockchain within the healthcare field deals with managing healthcare provider data. Consistent with the HIPAA Journal, the entire number of records compromised in healthcare data breaches in February 2020 amounted to almost 1,531,855. Therefore, blockchain is certainly a positive alternative for improving the safety of healthcare provider data while ensuring seamless data movement.

Synaptic Healthcare Alliance is the most notable example of using Quorum blockchain for the healthcare sector. The first objective of the Synaptic Healthcare Alliance project focuses on creating an industry-wide database for healthcare providers. The project aims to resolve the concerns related to healthcare provider data management. The uses of Quorum blockchain in Synaptic Healthcare Alliance highlight improving data quality and decreasing administrative costs. Synaptic Healthcare Alliance achieves these outcomes by distributing provider data inputs together with the modifications introduced by different participants throughout the blockchain network.

4. Digital Identity

Digital identity use cases are also among the important highlights among the answers to 'who is using

Quorum?' with Uqudo being a prominent example. It is a mobile-based identity management platform that helps customers shift the physical ID records and existing digital IDs to their phones. The appliance leverages NFC and biometrics for the verification of private information about a private. Additionally, Quorum could provide suitable proof regarding the integrity of digital IDs also as onboard documents.

Uqudo can support customers using phones to consume services from identity-based service providers. Users could easily avail of services like applying for telecommunication services, age verification in online shopping or providing the KYC details for opening a checking account. Uqudo helps users in creating a digital representation of ID details on mobile phones with a digital ID wallet. The ID wallet leverages the Quorum blockchain to offer a further security layer. Consequently, the uses of Quorum blockchain in digital identity could clearly deliver promising benefits with use cases involving consent management and data sharing.

5. Supply Chain

The wide selection of blockchain applications in supply chain management has recently gained promising attention. Actually, supply chain management provides better scope for various Quorum use cases. Quorum can support supply chain applications in various areas, including automated inventory and shipment tracking. Additionally, the utilization cases of Quorum blockchain in supply chain management also specialize in verifying the authenticity of luxury goods.

A dramatic example of supply chain tracking with the assistance of Quorum blockchain is Starbucks. It has successfully implemented Quorum alongside the Azure Blockchain Service of Microsoft for tracking the assembly of coffee. The Quorum blockchain use cases for supply chain tracking as well point to the instance of Eximchain. It is a protocol tailored for scalable and public blockchain networks to enable privacy across different enterprise supply chain applications. Renowned luxury goods brand, LVMH, has also started a Quorum blockchain-based solution for verifying the authenticity of luxury goods.

6. Governance and Public Sector

Quorum blockchain has also found many applications within the governance and public sector. An interesting example of a national network-supported Quorum blockchain is Alastria. It is actually the primarily regulated blockchain ecosystem within the world. Alastria includes quite 70 Spanish firms like Santander, University of Valencia, BBVA, Santander, University of Girona, Telefonica and therefore the University of Malaga. The project focuses on three separate pillars of blockchain technology,

- The Alastria Association
- The Alastria Network
- The Alastria ID

The Alastria Network is the blockchain infrastructure for Quorum blockchain in creating a national network.

The Alastria ID is the digital identity standard on the network. With the applications of Alastria, it can assist in encouraging collaboration between the private sector, the tutorial world, and public administration.

7. Enterprise Solutions

The capabilities of Quorum blockchain also are evidently useful for enterprise solutions. Quorum blockchain is a perfect instrument for offering support to optimize existing enterprise operations and processes. Speaking of Quorum enterprise solutions, three distinct use cases exist for improvising support with technology solutions.

First, ProofSuite is an example of using Quorum blockchain to empower financial technology research and development.

Another important example of using Quorum blockchain in enterprise solutions is BlockTEST. The appliance offers adequate support for the event and optimization of enterprise blockchain solutions. As a result, the appliance would enable improvements in finances, products, and data flow.

LayerX is another entry among Quorum blockchain's uses for enterprise support solutions. It leverages Quorum blockchain for offering technical consulting, security auditing, blockchain integration, and proof of concept development. Presently, the appliance has focused its attention on the Japanese market.

8. Media and Entertainment

Blockchain has also discovered many significant use cases within the field of media and entertainment. The instance of Xbox computer game Royalties showcases the potential of Quorum blockchain for streamlining rights management. Ernst and Young and Microsoft are presently performing on this blockchain solution supported Quorum blockchain.

The basic objective of Xbox computer game Royalties will specialize in reducing the time interval and ensuring faster tracking of royalties within the video gaming domain. With this application, Quorum blockchain showcases extraordinary advantages of improving trust and transparency among industry stakeholders. However, Quorum blockchain could offer the foremost interesting value proposal in managing operational inadequacies during the royalty management process.

9. Travel and Hospitality

Quorum blockchain use cases have also found their way into the domain of travel and hospitality. The primary example of use cases of Quorum within the retail travel and hospitality sector refers to EMR. The owner of Burj Khalifa, Emaar, has launched EMR as a platform for rewarding customers for business referrals and loyalty. The platform would reward EMR tokens, and users could redeem the tokens for malls, land, e-commerce operations, and hotels of Emaar. Additionally, It is also suitable for trading with other users. Another example of using Quorum blockchain for travel and hospitality is for airlines' refund payout. Travacoin, a digital payment system, uses the Quorum blockchain to ensure that airlines can efficiently provide passenger refunds and compensation.

10. Blockchain Data Analytics

The last use case example of Quorum blockchain presents a stimulating proposition because it is directly associated with Quorum. The Splunk App for Quorum may be a useful gizmo for monitoring the blockchain infrastructure developed on the Quorum blockchain. It can provide an in-depth impression of the building blocks as dashboards for ensuring visibility and monitoring of Quorum node logs. Quorum Splunk app also helps in recording metrics and transaction analytics from the blockchain network.

```solidity
pragma solidity >= 0.5.3;

import "./PermissionsUpgradable.sol";

/** @title Voter manager contract
  * @notice This contract holds implementation logic for all account voter and
    voting functionality. This can be called only by the implementation
    contract only. there are few view functions exposed as public and
    can be called directly. these are invoked by quorum for populating
    permissions data in cache
  * @dev each voting record has an attribute operation type (opType)
    which denotes the activity type which is pending approval. This can
    have the following values:
        0 - None - indicates no pending records for the org
        1 - New org add activity
        2 - Org suspension activity
        3 - Revoke of org suspension
        4 - Assigning admin role for a new account
        5 - Blacklisted node recovery
        6 - Blacklisted account recovery
  */
contract VoterManager {
    PermissionsUpgradable private permUpgradable;
    struct PendingOpDetails {
        string orgId;
        string enodeId;
        address account;
        uint256 opType;
    }

    struct Voter {
        address vAccount;
        bool active;
    }

    struct OrgVoterDetails {
        string orgId;
        uint256 voterCount;
        uint256 validVoterCount;
        uint256 voteCount;
        PendingOpDetails pendingOp;
        Voter [] voterList;
        mapping(address => uint256) voterIndex;
        mapping(uint256 => mapping(address => bool)) votingStatus;
    }

    OrgVoterDetails [] private orgVoterList;
    mapping(bytes32 => uint256) private VoterOrgIndex;
    uint256 private orgNum = 0;

    // events related to managing voting accounts for the org
    event VoterAdded(string _orgId, address _vAccount);
    event VoterDeleted(string _orgId, address _vAccount);
```

Figure 9- Example of Quorum Blockchain

How Does Quorum Achieve Consensus?

Another major question associated with Quorum is its approach to achieving consensus. Quorum depends on a majority voting protocol, referred to as QuorumChain. It features a subset of nodes within the network with the power to vote on the blocks. The voting role helps nodes vote on the precise blocks that should be selected as a canonical head at a selected height.

Block creation for Quorum blockchain is feasible only with nodes assigned the maker's role. The node with the maker role could generate a block and will sign it in a unique manner. Other nodes could verify that imported block; it is the signature of one of the nodes with permission to form blocks.

QuorumChain is beneficial for various Quorum blockchain use cases with its implementation within the sort of a sensible contract. The deployment of a smart contract is one of the essential factors for consensus management. Additionally, It is also provided an enhancement over the census-upgrade process.

The smart contract can track the lists of voters and block makers. Both the lists might be managed through straightforward and standard transactions. Therefore, users can get explicit control and clarity over the identity of people liable for network governance.

Data Privacy- The assets of Quorum

Quorum blockchain sells itself on the vow of privacy. Data privacy in Quorum is clearly apparent with the power of segmentation and cryptography. Cryptography is usually applicable for data within the transactions, visible for everybody on the blockchain. Segmentation is appropriate for the local state database of each node altogether uses of Quorum blockchain. The local stated database includes the contract storage, and only the node can access it.

The nodes involved in the private transactions can only ensure the execution of the private contract code. The concerned private contract code is said to the transactions that end in updates for the private contract data storage vested within the local state database. Thus, the local state database of every node is full of private and public data they are involved.

The Working of Quorum - Private Transactions and Smart Contracts

An API related to the dApp for creating the transaction helps in deploying the private transactions. A personal contract is essentially a contract supported by a personal transaction. The node related to private transactions would ensure the decryption of transaction data before sending it to the EVM.

The EVM does not specialize in supporting any encryption or decryption operations. Furthermore, the private state data associated with a personal contract rests within the local database of parties involved in the transaction. As a result, the various uses of Quorum blockchain are capable of offering restrictions on the availability of data external to the local node.

1. Privacy of Transactions

Quorum ensures transactions through an inventory of public keys capable of identifying the parties to a transaction. Therefore, they will ensure the transaction's privacy to the parties. Within the case of this list, the creation of a typical Ethereum transaction features a singular highlight.

The payload is essentially the hash function of the encrypted private data. The newly created transaction, including the cryptographic hash, only moves to the Quorum node. Next, it goes to all nodes throughout the network within the sort of a pending transaction.

The basic components of a Quorum transaction include the subsequent:

- Recipient information
- Signature of identification of the sender
- The amount of ether, however, ether balance is not mandatory with Quorum
- The optional data field, which contains a hash for personal transactions
- The optional list of parties related to a transaction

2. Private Contracts

Private contracts even have a profound role in the uses of Quorum blockchain. They are just contracts created through a personal transaction. The state of personal contracts has representation as a private Patricia-Merkle tree. It is impossible to ensure the creation of a personal contract with a public transaction. Why? The documentation for the state of the contract developed with public transactions must be during a different public state Patricia-Merkle tree.

Validation of Blocks and State Consensus

The standard Ethereum block validation process would offer a crucial step for confirming the worldwide position of various contracts aligning with the worldwide state hash related to the block header. This offers cryptographic proof that each node within the network has the proper same state database. The proof actually is a provable prototype.

The Quorum state database is a crucial component for Quorum uses with the power of two separate databases. The method for Quorum block validation would only match the general public state.

Conversely, parties related to a personal contract may need cryptographic state consensus evidence. It is a distributed application retrieving a specific block's private contract state hash. Additionally, it can help share the worth with the parties to the contract across on-chain and off-chain transactions. The precise application design could not need parties of an equivalent contract capable of possessing a special state. Public state consensus could ensure that parties with a personal transaction could not leave consensus for subsequent reasons.

Validation of a block by incorporating global transaction hash consensus also as public state consensus EVM is deterministic in nature, and therefore the same inputs are always capable of generating similar outputs.

Subsequently, It is unlikely for the EVM to get a singular state of personal contract through processing a personal transaction.

Chapter 10 - Risks and Challenges of Blockchain Technology

One of the main draws of blockchain technology is additionally one of its most vital challenges. Currently, there's little or no regulation regarding what's and is not allowed within the blockchain space. Due to this, there are numerous instances of hackers having the ability to form off with many dollars of investor money due to loopholes within the online blockchain systems. Despite the promise of security on the present blockchains, there are teething issues that hackers are taking advantage of to the detriment of each blockchain user (ALI, 2022).

Not long ago, there was a case with Enigma, a decentralized platform that was preparing to boost money through an ICO. Hackers were ready to hack Enigma's website and various social accounts successfully. This allowed the hackers to send spam to Enigma's community and make off almost $500,000. The Enigma project was launched by a gaggle of MIT graduates, who sent out invites for people to hitch the

Enigma community. The hackers grabbed money from those that joined the company's official list and Slack group. In all, there have been around 9,000 users and participants who were suffering from this security breach.

The hackers effectively posted messages on Slack, altered the official website, and spoofed emails to the community list to make it appear like the corporate was making a proper request for money. Participants of the community responded by sending money that was deposited directly into the hacker's crypto wallet.

Last year there was an identical hack but on a larger scale when the Decentralized Autonomous Organization or DAO, built on Ethereum, was hacked and resulted in a loss of $50 million to hackers.

The DAO was alleged to be a decentralized investment fund where decisions would not rest on just a couple of partners. Still, anyone invested within the fund must choose which companies or projects the corporation should invest in. It was found out that the more you simply contributed, the more votes you bought.

Nobody could take the cash and run away since the fund was built to be distributed. Unfortunately, thanks to human and programming errors, hackers were ready to exploit the system to receive a $50 million payday, which has not yet been recovered.

Another example of blockchain technology's challenges comes from a corporation called OneCoin. Recently, a corporation referred to as Gnosis sold $12..5 million worth of a token called GNO in only over ten minutes. The sale was intended to buy the event of a complicated prediction market. The initial coin offering, ICO, received enthusiastic reviews across the worldwide press.

On that same day, a corporation called OneCoin, based in Mumbai, India, was in the middle of a sales talk for its own digital currency when financial enforcement officers raided their offices.

Ultimately, eighteen OneCoin reps were jailed, and quite $2 million in investor funds were confiscated. Multiple authorities describe OneCoin as being hyped as the next bitcoin, as a Ponzi scheme. Before the corporate offices in Mumbai could be raided, they had already transferred at least $350 million in swindled funds.

Major Hurdles of Blockchain

Currently, there are significant hurdles within the way to formally legalizing and regulating crypto trades. Comparable challenges exist with market growth and adoption. A number of the problems surrounding blockchain include what sorts of tax structures are right for blockchain markets, the way to trace and aggregate funds, where spending and income information will come from, and how it will be gathered. As long as these problems remain, widespread adoption of blockchain technology will be difficult.

However, there's some promise for the longer-term use of blockchain technology. South Korea and Japan have made substantial advances recently, which will leave legal bitcoin transactions, and various applications have opened investment channels within the blockchain space to traditional investors. These advancements have led to an inflow of funds to different blockchain companies, which, in turn, are ready to invest in growth, research, and, therefore, promote their particular blockchain services.

Risks of Blockchain Technology

As a replacement technology, resolving challenges like transaction speed, the verification process, and data limits are standing within the way of creating blockchain widely adopted technology. Blockchain projects' regulatory status is also a risk of blockchain technology and is currently uncertain.

If financial institutions and governments do not invest in the thought of blockchain technology, or if It is pushed away due to a scarcity of clear guidelines on how the industry should be regulated, blockchain will certainly not gain the widespread adoption that investors and experts hope for, causing it to be a novelty idea and little more.

The mining of blocks is very energy intensive and is becoming even costlier with the creation of every new block on the chain. There may be a threshold to what miners are willing to spend to unravel mathematical puzzles to earn a couple of bitcoins as their reward.

Cybersecurity and integration concerns will need to be addressed before the overall public will be willing to trust their personal data to a blockchain solution. This also goes for approval from any body of users or a Board of Directors to form significant changes to or maybe completely replace an existing system.

Finally, there's the matter of social and cultural adoption of blockchain technology. Blockchain represents an entire shift to a decentralized network. This needs a big buy-in from all users and operators on the network. Also, since It is such a big development,

It is not entirely understood by a majority of the population. Will all of those risks and hurdles, it will be several years before we see widespread adoption of blockchain solutions.

Chapter 11 - Deciding if Blockchain Technology is a correct choice for You

The most common reasons that somebody might consider an experiment with blockchain may be a continuous desire to experiment with new technologies, a requirement for blockchain's timestamp technology, or an interest in the many various ways blockchain can safeguard existing data. Like any new technology, It is critical that you simply look before you leap and consider if blockchain technology is basically right for you and your business.

Know Who is going to be watching Your Data

In a majority of the normal centralized databases, anyone with access to that has their activities stored just in case they have to be reviewed later. You will enjoy employing a blockchain if you would like to possess many individuals who check out your data daily but do not need them to possess written access to the information. Employing a blockchain in your business may assist in streamlining the method by providing users with read-only access and having a log in a more traditional sense when It is required.

Writeable Data

An average user database is usually protected through a mixture of usernames and passwords and several levels of restricted access. You will then implement even more security measures to stop your high-level data from being accessed when it should not. Even with all those precautions, the quality blockchain security protocols still make it perfectly clear who created which blocks and, therefore, the time and place they created them.

These measures ensure that every transaction is usually completed with the complete knowledge of the creator, who can then confirm and approve the transaction. This, of course, assumes that the individuals are not adding information to the node. The signature is further confirmed before the block is often attached to the chain. Albeit a username and password combination is not required for users to possess access, the chain will still automatically record the IP address of any user who creates new blocks.

Data Alteration

If you think that you simply are getting to alter data that is being stored during a blockchain, then blockchain technology would not be right for you and your business. With a centralized database, it is simple to change data by merely tracking down the acceptable clearance, changing the specified data, and having those changes saved during a log. With blockchain technology, the sole way to do an equivalent with data that has already been stored is to simultaneously change the information across 51 percent of the nodes available on the network. While this is often a helpful security feature of blockchains, in some circumstances, it will automatically prohibit blockchain databases from running in several others.

Data Restoration

If you discover yourself doing nothing but updating backup data, then you would possibly discover blockchain technology beneficial. Once you use a standard database, you've got to manually instigate backups, leaving you to stress about ensuring everything is where it must be. On the other hand, when it involves a distributed database, the knowledge is automatically updated across all available nodes whenever new information is added to the chain. As long as all of your nodes do not catastrophically fail at an equivalent time, then you do not have anything to stress about.

Depending on the prices related to backing up and updating your data, you will find that the extra operating expenses related to a decentralized database may make it the low-cost alternative of the two.

Easy to Share

Centralized databases are often restricted concerning access, while a blockchain database is often temporarily connected to a different blockchain database easily. This ability to attach to other blockchain databases makes the method of transferring information between the two nearly painless.

The other blockchains that you simply are connecting to might be associated with a selected department within your company or maybe associated with completely different companies. If you are thinking doing this, it is important to remember that once you grant someone access to your blockchain, you are providing them access to your whole blockchain. This might require significant getting to utilize if you affect sensitive information effectively.

Storage Limitations

One area where a standard database beats a blockchain database is within the amount of knowledge which will be comfortably stored.

Everything on the blockchain is downloaded when a replacement node is made during a decentralized database. Alongside the fact that nodes are often thousands and thousands of miles aside from each other, this means It is in your best interest to keep the entire amount of knowledge in your blockchain manageable. As a point of reference, the database for bitcoin only has about 100 gigabytes, and It has been around for nearly ten years. If you would like a high-capacity option, you would possibly should look elsewhere.

Verification Process

If you are planning on running a personal blockchain, then you do not have to worry about funding a gift for the validation of blocks. In fact, you will not even need to worry about a few proof of labor system in the least.

Instead, you will want to use a symbol of stake model because everyone within the private blockchain will have a stake to keep the chain up-to-date and reliable. This suggests that the method for validating blocks is often more straightforward. However, you will still have to think about the quantity of your time it will take and ensure that you've got the workforce to facilitate the work.

Taking subsequent Step

After analyzing the specifics, if you opt to take advantage of blockchain technology, It is crucial that you simply consider exactly how you propose using the technology.

Suppose you are an existing business owner who hopes to urge before the curve. In that case, you will want to focus your attention and energy on the potential ways in which blockchain and smart technology can work together to enhance the ancillary aspects of your business. More specifically, you will want to require an extended check out things that have the potential to decrease costs and improve efficiency.

This means that you simply will need to consider all the various ways in which utilizing blockchain will cause you to be more competitive within the eyes of your competition by allowing you to urge a jump start on emerging trends in your industry.

Alternately, you will have to consider the varied disruptions to how your business works that implementing blockchain technology might bring to light.

This will require you to maneuver things around now in order that the disruptions you would possibly experience are kept to a minimum. Being conscious of what's likely to happen next will make it tons easier to face head-on.

If you are considering forming a replacement business based on blockchain, you will want to figure out as many blockchains as possible. This may assist you in enhancing your grasp of the technology and help form the technology more mainstream, which is what brand spanking new blockchain companies require.

If you hope to enter into the mainstream with the assistance of blockchain, you will want to do everything you will to ensure blockchain technology becomes mainstream.

You also want to remember that It is quite likely a troublesome road to travel. However, many of the foremost significant benefits of blockchain technology are only available to companies with existing infrastructure already in situ to take full advantage of them.

This means that the foremost realistic forecast for the increase of blockchain technology is that there'll be a couple of companies that are getting to come along and grab a share of the spotlight, leaving the remainder of the space at the highest being haunted by the members of the faction who can get their acts together and make an advance blockchain technology before their competition.

Chapter 12 - Blockchain Implementation Mistakes to Avoid

With all the hype surrounding blockchains, it is often easy to leap into the fray without watching how to implement your own blockchain distribution system. This is often an enormous mistake. Before you take the plunge, you would like to ensure that you simply avoid subsequent errors (Panetta, 2019).

Having Unrealistic Expectations
If you are planning on having the ability to use a blockchain efficiently, the primary thing you simply got to understand is that It is not a catchall solution to each problem. Fortunately, you will found out a personal

system, and only a couple of individuals will need to know if the initial testing goes badly.

This also goes for the quantity of data that is routinely stored in each block. The majority of the whole blockchain will ultimately be duplicated to every new node created, so a particularly bloated chain will be adding unnecessary bloat to all or any of the computers using the blockchain. It is essential to remember that the whole bitcoin blockchain is merely 55 gigs. While this is often great when it involves storing private databases securely, It is not the simplest choice when it involves the usage of large-scale data. A centralized data storage system will be the higher choice in these cases.

It is also important to recollect that while blockchain systems have numerous fail-safes in situ to stop user error, it does not suggest that they are infallible. Since a hash key merely mentions each block, humans are far more likely to mistake blocks for other blocks to everyone's detriment. So, if you are getting to utilize blockchains in your business, you would like to make certain to implement a failsafe to see for this type of thing to possess the best results.

Underestimating the Time Commitment

It will take tons of your time to understand blockchain technology's intricacies fully. If you propose seeing the implementation of a blockchain system through to completion, you've got to know precisely what proportion of time is required to utilize blockchain technology to its fullest potential. After reading this book, you will still have to do more research to know the simplest way to implement a blockchain that best serves the needs of your business. This suggests that you will need to understand what you are getting to be using blockchains daily and what any secondary or tertiary duties might include.

Only after you've got a transparent idea of what you are getting to be using the blockchain system will you be ready to determine which kind of creation software is right for you and your needs. The marketplace for blockchain creation tools is not crowded, which suggests you would like to understand exactly what you are trying to find regarding finding one that is reliable and effective. Making a poor decision on this may make the creation process harder than it must be.

Being Impatient

After you've got a transparent understanding of how you are getting to use your blockchain distributed database and the way you are getting to implement the blockchain, It is essential that you simply not hurry to end the method. When it involves implementing blockchain technology, you've got to require things at a more measured pace. The method is often long and sophisticated, but you want to follow it through to the letter and test it thoroughly before you start to believe the blockchain in a real-world setting. Fixing an honest blockchain takes time, and rushing will only cause issues.

Remember, it is important that you simply choose a timetable that accurately reflects how long it will take you to finish the project. It would be best to consider the time it will take to get buy-in from anyone else whose opinion is required before you start the method.

Not Limiting Access

When it involves exciting new technologies like blockchain, It is natural for varied people to be interested in testing it out. If you are running a personal blockchain, then it is crucial that you not let too many people have access until they have received appropriate training. Your young blockchain can become easily derailed if you permit even a few inexperienced users to assist. When it involves accessing the core of the blockchain during a private system, you would like to make certain to store the key for personal access that is generated with a replacement blockchain in a safe place because if it is lost, there'll be no way for you to regain control of the blockchain.

Conclusion

Few inventions and discoveries d over the course of history have had a long-lasting impact on the pace and direction of human progress. Blockchain technology has the potential to be one such invention.

The promise that it holds for redefining aviation, ocean freight, and global logistics and what it can do to rework healthcare by providing safe and secure medical records, also because of the opportunities within the fields of microfinance, finance, credit investments, and prediction markets, suggests that the planet is slowly awakening to what blockchain technology can do.

The capabilities of this developing technology are still being determined, and there's still tons of labor that also must be done. Many dollars in investments are being poured into this area of research and development, and each day we see new blockchain-based initiatives, ideas, and startups being launched, with all hoping to be the one in which will erupt and change the future of how things are accomplished.

The time for a shift is now, and new blockchain technology is driving the way. However, as we move forward, we'd like to require prudent steps to make certain that we correctly use the technology and deliver the maximum benefit to as many of us as possible.

Suppose you are considering utilizing blockchain technology for your business. In that case, the sole way you will truly master It is if you dedicate yourself to becoming a lifelong learner within the space.

Additional Learning Resources

Online Training

Online Degree™ in Blockchain
https://www.blockchain-council.org/online-degree/online-degree-blockchain/

Online Degree™ in Blockchain is designed to equip you with a profound knowledge of Blockchain technology. Backed by the extensive practical-based sessions, completing this blockchain degree ensures you the required competence to have a successful career in the Blockchain sphere.

As Blockchain technology has taken the digital world by storm, the future of Blockchain technology is promising. Becoming a master in Blockchain technology by going through Online Degree™ in Blockchain unfolds the world of opportunities for you.

After completing this Online Degree™, you will master the various aspects of blockchain technology, such as designing a blockchain network, blockchain architecture, deploying blockchain for real-world applications, and many more.

Online Degree™ in Blockchain for Business
https://www.blockchain-council.org/online-degree/blockchain-for-business/

Blockchain is lately gaining an immense reputation for its industry-disrupting capabilities. As a technology that simplifies complex business processes, a blockchain is a must-know tool in today's context. Online Degree-Blockchain for Business will give you the essential skills to leverage blockchain to increase business potential.

Master the core concepts of blockchain, offered to you through comprehensive modules and transform you into a sought-after blockchain professional.

After completing this course, business professionals can make informed business decisions pertaining to Blockchain proof-of-concept implementations.

Certified Blockchain Expert™
https://www.blockchain-council.org/certifications/certified-blockchain-professional-expert/

The Certified Blockchain Expert program has a comprehensive curriculum that will introduce you to the various facets of Blockchain technology and the growing industry. The certification will also assist you in understanding Blockchain-based business applications.

This training program will walk you through the various components of Blockchain technologies and how they affect enterprise imperatives. In addition, you will learn how to interact with business executives in a practical way and match their needs with pragmatic and immediately effective solutions, with decentralization at their heart. Overall, this certification will offer you a significant competitive advantage.

Certified Blockchain Expert™ is for anyone who wants to learn everything there is to know about enterprise Blockchains and how they may be used in the sector they wish to work.

After completing this Blockchain certification, you will master the core concepts of Blockchain technology that are commonly used across multiple industries to solve large-scale problems.

Certified Blockchain Architect™

https://www.blockchain-council.org/certifications/certified-blockchain-architect/

Blockchain Architects design blockchain solutions and define infrastructure as well as security requirements. They convert business needs into technical specifications and determine the parameters for tracking the solution's performance. A blockchain architect's job is to make rational decisions in challenging areas such that the implemented system adheres to the non-functional requirements.

With the aid of this certification, Blockchain Architects will be better able to use their theoretical and practical knowledge and get hands-on experience with all areas of Blockchain development. It will serve as a demonstration of your experience in the blockchain industry. You will also have the necessary exposure to develop the skills necessary to decide wisely about various blockchain initiatives. As a Certified Blockchain

Architect, you will have an advantage when creating and constructing Blockchain-based solutions for corporations and enterprises.

Certified Smart Contract Developer™
https://www.blockchain-council.org/certifications/certified-smart-contract-developer/

A Certified Smart Contract Developer is a skilled professional who understands and knows what Smart Contracts are and how to program them for any Blockchain platform efficiently.

Certified Smart Contract Developer is a thorough training and exam-based program that aims to provide proof of knowledge to the certificate holder within the blockchain space.

Tech giants, private firms, enterprises, startups, and even the government sector, including federal agencies, are rushing to take advantage of the perceived benefits of the blockchain phenomenon. Earning this certification will entitle you to become a smart contract developer, an extremely in-demand skill in the international job market.

After completing this certification, you will be able to master the core concepts that are required for having a better hold on smart contract development, giving you a significant advantage in the professional space of the blockchain world.

Certified Blockchain and Finance Professional™
https://www.blockchain-council.org/certifications/certified-blockchain-finance-professional/

Certified Blockchain and Finance Professional™ training is primarily directed to guide an individual for creating solutions that can influence all the aspects of Finance. This training deals with the assimilation of knowledge on how Blockchain can be leveraged to speed up and streamline the procedure of cross-border payments and reduce the cost.

Blockchain is a disruptive technology which is presently deployed in various domains to optimize multiple processes. As the market for Blockchain professionals is increasing in the Finance Industry, this certification will show to be your competitive supremacy over others.

After completing this certification, you will master the core concepts of implementing Blockchain in Finance Industry to solve large-scale problems.

Certified Blockchain Security Expert (CBSE)
https://101blockchains.com/certification/certified-blockchain-security-expert/

The Certified Blockchain Security Expert (CBSE) certification is an innovative professional credential in the field of blockchain security. The CBSE certification is suitable for professionals who want to enhance their knowledge of blockchain security basics, alongside practical implications of blockchain threats and risks.

101 Blockchains created the CBSE certification as a credible addition to the portfolio of any security expert in the blockchain arena. Learners taking the CBSE certification training course will gain valuable knowledge of blockchain threat modeling and security assessments, alongside expanding their expertise in designing and developing secure distributed applications.

If you want to become a blockchain security expert, the CBSE certification offers the right set of skills and knowledge you need to achieve success.

Certified Enterprise Blockchain Architect (CEBA)
https://101blockchains.com/certification/certified-enterprise-blockchain-architect/

The Certified Enterprise Blockchain Architect (CEBA) certification is a popular job-centric blockchain credential with a specific focus on blockchain solution architecture. The CEBA certification is the best choice for any professional interested in designing blockchain-based systems and solutions.

The CEBA certification covers a broad range of topics related to blockchain development. Besides the concepts underlying blockchain architecture and development, the CEBA certification focuses on blockchain use cases and selecting suitable blockchain systems for enterprise needs.

The CEBA certification offers the best collection of learning resources for those who wish to become professional enterprise blockchain architects.

6-Figure Blockchain Developer

https://pro.eattheblocks.com/p/6-figure-blockchain-developer

Learn smart contracts and Dapp development for Ethereum

Part 1: Introduction to Blockchain and Ethereum

Part 2: Smart Contracts Development (Solidity 0.6)

Part 3: Build a rockstar portfolio of Blockchain projects:

Part 4: Find your First Blockchain Job using the "Aim, Load Fire" method

Become a Blockchain Developer

https://www.udacity.com/course/blockchain-developer-nanodegree--nd1309#related-nanodegrees

Demand for blockchain developers is skyrocketing. In this program, you will work with the Bitcoin and Ethereum protocols, build real-world applications, and gain the essential skills for a career in this dynamic space.

Certified Ethereum Expert™

https://www.blockchain-council.org/certifications/certified-ethereum-expert-cee/

Certified Ethereum Expert™ is an exclusively developed and expertly curated certification focusing on the core concepts of the Ethereum Blockchain. An Ethereum Expert is one who develops decentralized applications and protocols to improve fault tolerance and for processing of large chunks of data.

Validating and understanding your skills through this exhaustive exam-based certification will provide insights into the workings of Ethereum and the Smart Contracts. Successful completion of this certification will enable you to build Ethereum-based applications for enterprises and will brighten your chances to start a rewarding career in the Blockchain domain.

After completing this Certified Ethereum Expert™ Certification, you will master the core concepts of Ethereum Blockchain that are commonly used across multiple industries to build Decentralized Applications.

Certified Ethereum Developer™
https://www.blockchain-council.org/certifications/certified-ethereum-developer/

An Ethereum developer is one who has expertise in one of the best-decentralized blockchain platforms available today, Ethereum. The developer is fully equipped with the skills required to excel in the world of blockchain networks, having varied knowledge of the basics and advanced concepts of Ethereum. Earning this certification will entitle you to become an Ethereum developer, which is currently an extremely in-demand skill in the international job market.

After completing this certification, you will master the core concepts of Ethereum along with a greater understanding of Blockchains and Ethereum.

Certified Hyperledger Expert™

https://www.blockchain-council.org/certifications/certified-hyperledger-expert/

A Certified Hyperledger Expert is a skilled professional who understands what is hyperledger and how hyperledger works and uses the same knowledge to build private permissioned blockchain-based applications for enterprises, businesses, and research projects.

The CHE credential certifies an individual in the Hyperledger discipline of distributed ledger technology from a vendor-neutral perspective. Certified Hyperledger Expert is especially for people who want to begin learning about Hyperledger technology. This course will cover all the details regarding hyperledger fabric architecture and composer. It will also help you to understand the hyperledger family, so you can begin building blockchain applications on top of hyperledger platform.

After completing this Hyperledger certification, you will master the core concepts of Hyperledger Technology that are commonly used across multiple industries to solve large-scale problems.

Certified Quorum Expert™
https://www.blockchain-council.org/certifications/certified-Quorum-expert/

Quorum is one of the first significant steps towards universal adoption of Blockchain among financial industries. Quorum is an enterprise-focused, private-permissioned blockchain infrastructure specifically designed for commercial use cases. Quorum was intended to appease many of the critical concerns that financial institutions have regarding blockchains.

Certified Quorum Expert training and certification provides an introduction to Quorum Blockchain as it is a widely accepted Blockchain solution for organizations in various domains due to the performance, security, and governance. Being certified as a Quorum Expert will serve you well in terms of capturing new opportunities. It acts as a catalyst in accelerating your career growth in the field of Blockchain.

Completion of this certification will enable you to understand Quorum ecosystem, transaction mechanism, and consensus algorithms.

Certified Corda Expert™

https://www.blockchain-council.org/certifications/certified-corda-expert/

Corda blockchain platform is a revolutionary distributed ledger specifically designed for financial services' needs. Becoming a certified Corda Expert by earning Blockchain-Council's Certified Corda Expert

Certification is the key to a rewarding career in the Blockchain sphere.

Certified Corda expert training is an expertly curated and excellently designed training, rendering profound knowledge on various aspects of Corda blockchain platform. Getting certified as a Corda Expert will uplift your career.

After completing this certification, you will master the core concepts of the Corda platform.

Build a Blockchain and a Cryptocurrency from Scratch
Instructor: David Joseph Katz

https://www.udemy.com/course/build-blockchain/

What you will learn

1. Discuss the implementation of Blockchain and cryptocurrencies.

2. Understand main blockchain concepts like Proof-of-Work, mining, peer-to-peer connections, etc.
3. Build their own blockchain and cryptocurrency.
4. Create a NodeJS application with real-time WebSocket connections.
5. Build an API with NodeJS and Express.

Ethereum Blockchain Developer Bootcamp With Solidity (2022)

Created by Ravinder Deol, Thomas Wiesner, and Haseeb Chaudhry

https://www.udemy.com/course/blockchain-developer/

What you will learn

- Become Skilled In Solidity Programming By Building Projects.
- Grasp Blockchain Technology (Theoretical and Practical).
- Understand How Smart Contracts Work (Theoretical and Practical).

- Become Skilled Using The Core Development Tools Of Ethereum.
- Understand Ethereum Development Functions.
- Become Skilled In Advanced Development With Truffle.
- Grasp How Decentralised Technology Works.
- Understand The Structure Of Solidity Code.

Blockchain Development on Hyperledger Fabric using Composer

Instructor: Rajeev Sakhuja

https://www.udemy.com/course/hyperledger/

What you will learn

- Develop Hyperledger Blockchain Applications using Composer Framework
- Model the Blockchain Applications using Composer modeling language
- Evaluate if a business application will benefit by adoption of Distributed Ledger Technology

- Develop front-end (Client) applications using Composer API
- Leverage Composer REST Server to design a web-based Blockchain solution
- Describe the various components of Hyperledger Fabric Technology (Peers, Orderer, MSP, CA ...)
- Design Hyperledger Fabric Composer Business Network Application (NOT the infrastructure)

Books

Blockchain By Example: A developer's guide to creating decentralized applications using Bitcoin, Ethereum, and Hyperledger
https://www.amazon.com/Blockchain-Example-Decentralized-applications-Hyperledger/dp/1788475682/

Implement decentralized blockchain applications to build scalable Dapps

Key Features

- Understand the blockchain ecosystem and its terminologies
- Implement smart contracts, wallets, and consensus protocols
- Design and develop decentralized applications using Bitcoin, Ethereum, and Hyperledger

Mastering Blockchain: A deep dive into distributed ledgers, consensus protocols, smart contracts, DApps, cryptocurrencies, Ethereum, and more, 3rd Edition
https://www.amazon.com/Mastering-Blockchain-distributed-consensus-cryptocurrencies-dp-1839213191/dp/1839213191/

Develop a deeper understanding of what's under the hood of blockchain with this technical reference guide on one of the most disruptive modern technologies

Key Features

- Updated with four new chapters on consensus algorithms, Ethereum 2.0, tokenization, and enterprise blockchains
- Learn about key elements of blockchain theory such as decentralization, cryptography, and consensus protocols
- Get to grips with Solidity, Web3, cryptocurrencies, smart contract development, and solve scalability, security, and privacy issues
- Discover the architecture of different distributed ledger platforms, including Ethereum, Bitcoin, Hyperledger Fabric, Hyperledger Sawtooth, Corda, and Quorum

Blockchain with Hyperledger Fabric: Build decentralized applications using Hyperledger Fabric 2, 2nd Edition

https://www.amazon.com/Blockchain-Hyperledger-Fabric-decentralized-applications-ebook-dp-B08N5CJ6RR/dp/B08N5CJ6RR/

Learn to develop blockchain-based distributed ledgers and deploy a Hyperledger Fabric network with concrete exercises and examples

Key Features

- Updated with the latest features and additions that come with Hyperledger Fabric 2
- Write your own smart contracts and services using Java and JavaScript on a Hyperledger Fabric network
- Dive into real-world blockchain challenges such as integration and scalability

Blockchain Development with Hyperledger: Build decentralized applications with Hyperledger Fabric and Composer
https://www.amazon.com/Blockchain-Development-Hyperledger-decentralized-applications-dp-1838649980/dp/1838649980/

Learn quick and effective techniques for developing blockchain-based distributed ledgers with ease

Key Features

- Discover why blockchain is a game changer in the technology landscape
- Set up blockchain networks using Hyperledger Fabric
- Write smart contracts at speed with Hyperledger Composer

Hands-On Blockchain Development in 7 Days: Create a decentralized gaming application using Ethereum
https://www.amazon.com/Hands-Blockchain-Development-Days-decentralized/dp/183864010X/

Build an Ethereum gaming application from scratch in a span of seven days by mastering smart contracts in Solidity

Key Features

- Create a simple, functional decentralized application on the Ethereum network
- Learn fundamental blockchain programming concepts to become a blockchain developer
- Understand the development life cycle of a blockchain application

Mastering Blockchain: A deep dive into distributed ledgers, consensus protocols, smart contracts, DApps, cryptocurrencies, Ethereum, and more, 3rd Edition
https://www.amazon.com/Mastering-Blockchain-distributed-consensus-cryptocurrencies/dp/1839213191/

Develop a deeper understanding of what's under the hood of blockchain with this technical reference guide on one of the most disruptive modern technologies

Key Features

- Updated with four new chapters on consensus algorithms, Ethereum 2.0, tokenization, and enterprise blockchains
- Learn about key elements of blockchain theory such as decentralization, cryptography, and consensus protocols
- Get to grips with Solidity, Web3, cryptocurrencies, and smart contract development and solve scalability, security, and privacy issues
- Discover the architecture of different distributed ledger platforms, including Ethereum, Bitcoin, Hyperledger Fabric, Hyperledger Sawtooth, Corda, and Quorum

Blockchain Development for Finance Projects: Building next-generation financial applications using Ethereum, Hyperledger Fabric, and Stellar
https://www.amazon.com/Blockchain-Development-Finance-Projects-next-generation/dp/1838829091/

A practical blockchain handbook designed to take you through implementing and re-engineering banking and financial solutions and workflows using eight step-by-step projects

Key Features

- Implement various end-to-end blockchain projects and learn to enhance present-day financial solutions
- Use Ethereum, Hyperledger, and Stellar to build public and private decentralized applications
- Address complex challenges faced in the BFSI domain using different blockchain platform services

Hands-On Cybersecurity with Blockchain: Implement DDoS protection, PKI-based identity, 2FA, and DNS security using Blockchain

https://www.amazon.com/Hands-Cybersecurity-Blockchain-Implement-protection/dp/1788990188/

Develop blockchain application with step-by-step instructions, working examples, and helpful recommendations

Key Features

- Understanding blockchain technology from the cybersecurity perspective
- Developing cyber security solutions with Ethereum blockchain technology
- Understanding real-world deployment of blockchain-based applications

Blockchain Quick Start Guide: A beginner's guide to developing enterprise-grade decentralized applications

https://www.amazon.com/Blockchain-Quick-Start-Guide-enterprise-grade/dp/1789807972/

Learn quick and effective techniques to get up and running with building blockchain, including Ethereum and Hyperledger Fabric.

Key Features

- Understand the key concepts of decentralized applications and consensus algorithms
- Learn key concepts of Ethereum and Solidity programming
- A practical guide to getting started with building efficient Blockchain applications with Ethereum and Hyperledger

Learn Blockchain Programming with JavaScript: Build your very own Blockchain and decentralized network with JavaScript and Node.js

https://www.amazon.com/Learn-Blockchain-Programming-JavaScript-decentralized/dp/1789618827/

Explore the essentials of blockchain technology with JavaScript to develop highly secure bitcoin-like applications

Key Features

- Develop bitcoin and blockchain-based cryptocurrencies using JavaScript
- Create secure and high-performant blockchain networks
- Build custom APIs and decentralized networks to host blockchain applications

Building Blockchain Projects: Building decentralized Blockchain applications with Ethereum and Solidity
https://www.amazon.com/Building-Blockchain-Projects-decentralized-applications/dp/178712214X/

Develop real-time practical DApps using Ethereum and JavaScript

Key Features

- Create powerful, end-to-end applications for Blockchain using Ethereum
- Write your first program using the Solidity programming language
- Change the way you think and design your applications by using the all-new database-Blockchain

Bibliography

@wackerow. (2022, June 16). *PROOF-OF-STAKE (POS)*. Retrieved from ethereum.org: https://ethereum.org/en/developers/docs/consensus-mechanisms/pos/

ALI, F. (2022, June 17). *The Top 6 Problems With Blockchain Technology*. Retrieved from www.makeuseof.com: https://www.makeuseof.com/problems-with-blockchain-technology/

Bashir, I. (2018). *Mastering Blockchain Second Edition.* Packt Publishing.

Bashir, I. (2020). *Mastering Blockchain: A deep dive into distributed ledgers, consensus protocols, smart contracts, DApps, cryptocurrencies, Ethereum, and more, 3rd Edition.* Packt Publishing .

Bellaj Badr, R. H. (2018). *Blockchain By Example: A developer's guide to creating decentralized applications using Bitcoin, Ethereum, and Hyperledger.* Packt Publishing.

Blockchain - Benefits, Drawbacks and Everything You Need to Know. (n.d.). Retrieved from marutitech.com: https://marutitech.com/benefits-of-blockchain/

Chen, J. L. (2021). *A Brief History of Cryptocurrencies and Blockchain.* Independently published .

Dr. Seok-Won Lee, I. S. (2021). *Blockchain Technology for IoT Applications (Blockchain Technologies).* Springer.

Harvey, C. R. (2021). *DeFi and the Future of Finance 1st Edition.* Wiley.

Jai Singh Arun, J. C. (2019). *Blockchain for Business.* Addison-Wesley Professional.

Lawton, G. (2022, March 24). *Top 9 blockchain platforms to consider in 2022.* Retrieved from techtarget.com: https://www.techtarget.com/searchcio/feature/Top-9-blockchain-platforms-to-consider

Marcelo Corrales Compagnucci, M. F. (2021). *Smart Contracts: Technological, Business and Legal Perspectives .* Hart Publishing.

Panetta, K. (2019, July 1). *7 Common Mistakes in Enterprise Blockchain Projects.* Retrieved from www.gartner.com/: https://www.gartner.com/smarterwithgartner/top-10-mistakes-in-enterprise-blockchain-projects

Roy, I. (2020). *Blockchain Development for Finance Projects: Building next-generation financial applications using Ethereum, Hyperledger Fabric, and Stellar.* Packt Publishing.

Shelper, P. (2019). *Blockchain Loyalty: Disrupting loyalty and reinventing marketing using blockchain and cryptocurrencies. 2nd Edition* . Loyalty & Reward Co.

Statista Research Department. (2022, June 7). *crypto-funds*. Retrieved from www.statista.com: https://www.statista.com/topics/7573/crypto-funds/

Weston, G. (2022, May 20). *blockchain-career-path*. Retrieved from 101blockchains.com: https://101blockchains.com/blockchain-career-paths/

Index

Bit Gold 24, 25, 95
Bitcoin 16, 19, 69, 72, 85, 86, 89, 94, 125, 137, 226, 235, 236, 237, 241
blockchain 14, 16, 17, 20, 26, 28, 29, 30, 32, 33, 34, 35, 39, 40, 41, 42, 43, 44, 45, 46, 47, 48, 49, 50, 51, 52, 53, 54, 55, 56, 58, 59, 60, 61, 62, 63, 64, 65, 66, 67, 68, 69, 71, 72, 74, 75, 77, 78, 79, 80, 81, 82, 85, 86, 88, 89, 91, 92, 95, 97, 98, 99, 102, 106, 111, 112, 117, 118, 119, 120, 125, 129, 130, 131, 132, 133, 134, 135, 136, 137, 138, 141, 142, 145, 146, 150, 151, 152, 153, 154, 155, 156, 157, 158, 161, 162, 163, 164, 165, 168, 169, 170, 171, 172, 173, 175, 176, 177, 178, 179, 180, 181, 182, 183, 184, 185, 186, 188, 189, 191, 192, 195, 197, 198, 199, 200, 201, 202, 203, 204, 205, 206, 207, 208, 209, 210, 211, 212, 213, 214, 215, 216, 217, 218, 220, 221, 222, 223, 224, 225, 226, 227, 228, 229, 230, 231, 232, 233, 235, 236, 237, 238, 239, 240, 241, 242, 243, 244, 245
B-Money 2, 22
bookkeeping 41
chaincode 133, 138, 139, 145, 149
cloud 45, 55, 66, 118
Consortium blockchains .. 33
Crowdlending 40
cryptocurrency 18, 19, 20, 35, 44, 67, 69, 71, 75, 77, 85, 86, 88, 89, 90, 92, 117, 123, 125, 126, 137, 233
decentralized 16
Decentralized Autonomous Organization 104, 196
Decentralized finance 85, 128
DigiCash 2, 20, 21
digital currency . 16, 86, 103, 118, 120, 129, 165, 197
digital ledgers 26
e-gold 22, 23
electoral system 101
encryption 18, 170, 190
energy 72, 105, 200, 207
ERC 2.0 103
Ethereum 16, 42, 60, 61, 66, 71, 74, 75, 76, 78, 85, 86, 87, 89, 91, 100, 103, 117, 118, 119, 120, 121, 124, 125, 126, 127, 128, 129, 130, 134, 138, 163, 164, 170, 171, 172, 174, 191, 193, 196, 226, 227, 228, 229, 233, 234, 235, 236, 237, 239, 240, 241, 242, 243, 244, 246, 247
fantasy sports 46, 47
financial industry 39

Gaming 46
Hashcash 21, 22, 24
Hyperledger 60, 131, 133, 134, 135, 136, 137, 138, 140, 141, 145, 146, 148, 229, 230, 234, 235, 236, 237, 238, 239, 241, 242, 244
immutable ... 27, 82, 85, 101, 106, 107, 137, 154
insurance 31, 50, 90, 98, 100, 105, 129, 152, 175, 177
IoT devices 43
legal contracts 43
multiple peers 141
music 33, 105, 129
Private blockchains .. 33
Public blockchains ... 33
Satoshi Nakamoto .. 16, 28, 89
Smart Contracts 94, 96, 98, 101, 104, 105, 107, 109, 115, 124, 138, 190, 221, 226, 227, 233
supply chain 48, 50, 175, 181
voting 101, 102, 130, 170, 188

About the Author

Matthew Smith is a lifelong technophile with over twenty years of experience in the IT industry. Matthew has a wide range of skills, from component-level repair to designing enterprise-level programs.

Matthew holds an associate of science in Electronics, an honors bachelor of science in IT, a degree in Blockchain, and currently pursuing an MBA. During his career, Matthew has held over 15 industry certifications. Currently holds the following certifications:

- Certified Chief Information Security Officer (CCISO)
- Information Systems Security Management Professional (CISSP-ISSMP)
- Certified Information Systems Security Professional (CISSP)

- Certified Enterprise Blockchain Architect (CEBA)
- Certified Strategy Director (CSD)

Regarding the future of Blockchain, Matthew believes that Blockchain is on the threshold of changing how organizations conduct business.

Dedication

This book is dedicated to my wonderful wife, who has provided me with love, companionship, and laughter throughout the years.

CPSIA information can be obtained
at www.ICGtesting.com
Printed in the USA
BVHW090229170922
647223BV00003B/75